G.C.E. EXAMINATION PAPERS
FOR TRANSLATION

General Editor: JOSÉ PICAZO

G.C.E. EXAMINATION PAPERS FOR TRANSLATION

General Editor: JOSÉ PICAZO

FRENCH EDITION *annotated by* W. C. DARWELL, M.A., M.Ed.

ITALIAN EDITION *annotated by*
RITA L. BLANCHARD TESSADORI, Dr. Lett. (Rome)

SPANISH EDITION *annotated by* JOSÉ PICAZO

Ordinary and Advanced Levels

G.C.E. EXAMINATION PAPERS
FOR TRANSLATION
Italian Edition

COMPILED BY

JOSÉ PICAZO
Formerly Principal Lecturer in Spanish, Liverpool Polytechnic

ANNOTATED BY

RITA L. BLANCHARD TESSADORI Dr. Lett. (Rome)
Housemistress, Garrett Green School, London

HODDER AND STOUGHTON
LONDON SYDNEY AUCKLAND TORONTO

ISBN 0 340 06787 X

First published 1960
Eighth impression 1976
Notes copyright © 1960 Rita L. Blanchard Tessadori

Printed in Great Britain for Hodder and Stoughton
Educational, a division of Hodder and Stoughton Ltd,
London, by Biddles Ltd, Guildford, Surrey

FOREWORD

THESE papers were originally set during the last few years by the University of London for the General Certificate of Education examinations in French, Spanish, German and Italian. They are here annotated for translation into Italian and are divided into two sections of forty passages each for Ordinary and Advanced Levels respectively.

I hope that this publication may be of assistance to teachers and students in Public and Grammar Schools, Evening Institutes and Colleges, both in the classroom and as homework. Acknowledgments are due to the Senate of the University of London for their kindness in granting permission to reproduce all the English passages set by that University for their General Certificate of Education examinations.

J. P.

PREFACE

THE notes which appear after the passages are designed to help students over difficulties of grammar, construction of phrases and vocabulary which, in the opinion of the author, need explanation or special emphasis.

The aim is to give assistance on points not normally fully explained in grammars or dictionaries, so as to prevent students from making errors and to guide them towards the acquisition of a feeling for the language.

The notes insist on the correct use of the tenses of the verb, of prepositions and of idiomatic expressions, encouraging a free translation where a literal one is impossible. Translations and comments are generally given once only and students are expected to learn and remember them. It is therefore advisable to work the passages in the given order. Occasionally, however, the more important grammatical rules are referred back to the passage and line where they are first fully commented upon.

R. L. B. T.

CONTENTS

"O" AND "A" LEVEL EXAMINATION
PAPERS FOR TRANSLATION

SECTION I

ORDINARY LEVEL

I

Last year Jack spent a few weeks with his uncle, who is a farmer. Jack had never been on a farm before, so he found everything that he saw very interesting. On weekdays he got up early and spent many hours in the open air, as he either played in the garden or helped his uncle in the fields. All the people were very busy, but in winter, when the ground was covered with snow, they did not work in the fields every day.

One morning they drove to the neighbouring town; it was market day, and the farmer bought some horses there. On the way home they passed through a small village and stopped to look at an old church surrounded by trees. Jack was pleased when they got home at last, for it was late and he was tired. He went to bed at once and was soon fast asleep.

II

The policemen looked at the peasant. "Here are twenty francs for your duck," went on Alain. "Will you accept?" The peasant hesitated but after a few moments he took the money, put it in his pocket and said to the policemen, "Let us go back to the village."

After their departure Maurice came out of the wood, still holding the duck, his fingers burnt. "I thought it was a wild duck," he said, and after putting back the

11

bird into the pot he sat down beside Alain. The next
10 day the boys decided to leave their camp.

They would set out before midday and would follow
the road through the forest. Alain went to say good-bye
to his friends at the farm, but the others remained at
the camp in order to work. When Alain came back at
15 eleven o'clock, everything was ready.

III

When Albert entered the office, nobody was working:
all the clerks were still talking about the lottery. Jules,
his best friend, held in his hand the newspaper in which
he had just read the list of the winning numbers. "I've
5 won nothing," he said. "Have you any tickets?"

"I bought one," answered Albert, "but I don't remember where I put it. I think I've lost it." As he
spoke, he took out his wallet and opened it: he noticed
immediately a piece of blue paper in one of the little
10 pockets. "No, I spoke too soon," he said. "Here it is.
Lend me your newspaper." Whilst he was reading the
list, the others continued their conversation. Suddenly,
from a corner of the room, they heard a strange cry.
It was Albert, who had become dreadfully pale. "Are
15 you ill?" Jules asked him. "No! I'm rich!" exclaimed
Albert. "I've won the big prize!"

IV

Croesus asked this question because he thought himself the most fortunate man in the world. But Solon,
who did not like to flatter people and who only knew
the language of truth, answered him:

"Yes, Sir, I have seen a very happy man called Tello 5
the Athenian."

The king was astonished and again repeated: "And
for what reason did you judge him the happiest of all?"

"For two reasons, Sir," Solon answered him; "the
first, because he saw his country flourishing, his sons 10
prosperous, all of them good men; and the other because
having such good fortune in this world, he went out to
fight bravely for his country and helped to drive out its
enemies."

Croesus' curiosity was aroused by this unexpected 15
reply, and he began to think of other questions that he
could ask him.

V

The train arrived soon after three o'clock. It was still
early, and Hans decided to leave his luggage at the
station. His aunt worked in the afternoon, so that he
had more than two hours for his walk through the town.
First he stood in front of the station and watched the 5
cars and the people who were hurrying across the street.
He waited here for some minutes, then he walked to the
big, old church which stood not far from his aunt's house.
The shops in the broad streets were larger than at
home, and for an hour he looked at the fine things in the 10
windows. "Good-day, Hans," said a voice behind him.
It was Aunt Lotte with many large parcels, which she
immediately gave to her nephew.

VI

Robert rang and the maid came. She told him that
the box had not been left behind by a preceding guest;
it had been brought with his own luggage. He went to

13

the theatre, where he met a friend to whom he related
5 his adventure. "What is in the box?" asked the friend.
"I don't know," answered Robert. "You should have
opened it," said his friend.

The whole evening he could not stop thinking about
the mysterious box. When the play was finished, he
10 walked back to his hotel. Having arrived there, he
wanted to have a look at the box, and carried it in front
of his fire. It was light, long and black, and had no
handle. While looking at it, he suddenly felt a strong
desire to open it. He broke the lock with his penknife;
15 what he saw inside filled him with horror.

VII

Nanette sat down on the wooden bench which stood
near the telephone; she was sure now that Jean was
in danger but that he was still alive. "The others
will find him," she said to herself, and she went into
5 the kitchen to prepare the meal of which she had
spoken.

Towards nine o'clock she heard footsteps on the path.
Putting down her knife, she ran to the door and opened
it. Several men were approaching the house, led by
10 Pierre, who was carrying a lamp in his hand. There
were five of them; it was evident that they had been
walking quickly.

Pierre explained that he had succeeded in finding all
the guides except Alfred. "He will come soon," he
15 added, "his wife will tell him we need him." They discussed their plans for a long time. They would set out
as soon as possible, and they would look for Jean at
first near La Brèche.

VIII

Bernard and his two sisters had sat down to table about half past one. Françoise, who had not said a word since the beginning of the meal, suddenly pushed back her plate.

"I cannot eat anything. I am not hungry." 5

Then, to the great surprise of her brother and sister, she added: "Have you ever heard of the Green Isle? It is somewhere in the middle of the river near Blaye."

Bernard reflected for a few moments. "Blaye?" he said. "The name is not unknown to me. There is a 10 map in the office. I will go and fetch it." He got up and went out of the dining-room.

A few minutes later he came back carrying the map. "There is the island you are speaking about," he said, putting the map on the table, "but why do you want to 15 know where it is?"

"Well," answered Françoise, "in his letter Father tells us he has bought that island and is having a house built there!"

IX

Nora was very angry because her friend did not believe her. She decided to prove that what she had said was true. She determined to drive the carriage home herself. She had always wanted to learn to drive, but the coachman had refused to teach her, saying that no 5 girl was old enough to drive till she was fifteen. Here was an opportunity to show what she could do.

A few moments before, she had been sorry that the coachman was not waiting for her, but now she hoped he would not come back too soon. She untied the horse, 10

jumped into the carriage, shouted good-bye to her
friend, and drove off very quickly. She had often
watched the coachman, and was sure she would be able
to imitate him. She was very proud to be driving the
15 carriage alone. What a pity, she thought, that her
father was not watching her.

X

The traveller had to get up very early on the following morning to catch the train that leaves Seville at
daybreak. Therefore he said to the innkeeper before
going to bed: "Wake me at half past four tomorrow
5 morning".

During the night, some students who were at the inn,
decided to play a joke and, entering the bedroom where
the traveller and the negro were, covered the traveller's
face with burnt cork, so that it appeared that both men
10 were black.

Then they knocked very loudly on the door shouting
that the inn was on fire. But both men went on sleeping
soundly. At last, however, the traveller awoke and,
jumping out of bed, looked at his face in a mirror.

15 "What a fool the innkeeper is!" he cried, "he has
awakened the negro instead of me!"

XI

The poor man was astonished because at that time
the Alcalde was well known and a very important person, and he began to tremble.

But the Secretary said to him: "Be calm," and they
5 both left the shop and made their way towards the
Residence which was not very far away.

As soon as the shoemaker presented himself, the

Alcalde said to him with great kindness:—

"My friend, I will begin by embracing you as a proof of my gratitude, and then I will repay you a debt that I 10 have owed you for many years."

The workman did not know what to say or do, and could scarcely believe what he heard.

But the Alcalde continued: "A good deed is never lost. I promised to remember your goodness to me. 15 Ask me what favour you wish, and if it is in my power, I shall grant it."

XII

The children arrived in London late in the evening; it was their first visit to the big city. Early next morning Charles was standing in the garden and looking up at the window of the room where his sister slept.

After he had whistled softly, a face appeared at the 5 open window. "Betty," said Charles, "I should like to go for a walk before breakfast." "I'm looking for my gloves," answered Betty. While he was waiting, Charles took an apple from his pocket and ate it.

When Betty came into the garden, the boy said that 10 they had no time to lose. At that moment the garden gate was opened by the postman, and the children ran out into the street as fast as they could.

XIII

After walking for an hour the doctor and his companion arrived at the peasant's cottage. They went in, and found the sick man lying on a poor bed in a corner. The doctor wasted no time. He took off his coat and began to examine his patient. The old woman's son 5 was obviously very ill.

"Why didn't you fetch me before?" he asked. "When did he fall ill?"

"Well, last Thursday he had to go to Cortillo," she
10 said. "It rained, and he got wet. He did not return home until about ten o'clock, and it was very cold by then. The next day he did not feel well, and on Sunday he seemed worse. This morning I thought he was dying, and I got up early and went to see you."
15 "First bring me hot water and clean towels. If only we were near a hospital!"

XIV

María went to school. She dared not stay away, as her brother would have discovered it and would have been curious. She had to sit there for the whole afternoon, almost without hearing the teachers or noticing
5 the change of lessons. How glad she was when the bell rang and classes were over! She wished to be alone and, avoiding her friends, she hurried into the street. It was six o'clock, and José used to expect her towards seven. What was she to do? Since her father's death
10 she had lived with José and his wife, but she wanted to go away to her aunt in Cadiz. For a year she had saved money . . . and now this difficulty! "Who can help me?" she wondered. "I know, I will go and see Carmen. I'm sure she will be able to think of something."

XV

"Good-bye, mother, I want to visit Peter Geyer this evening. He must be ill, because he was not at school today." George quickly put on his coat and hurried along the quiet road to his friend's house. When he
5 arrived, Peter's mother let him in and told him that her

son was in bed. "But you can go up to his room," she said.

The two boys spoke about the film which they had seen during the holidays. Shortly afterwards Mrs. Geyer came in. She had brought a cup of coffee and a large piece of cake for George and a glass of milk for Peter. The boys thanked her. Although Peter was ill, he quickly drank his milk and asked for something to eat.

XVI

The windows were open when Louis entered the bedroom, but he closed them at once, for night had already fallen. After pushing his suitcase under the bed, he went down to the dining-room and sat down at an empty table. One of the servants came towards him.

"Are you dining alone, sir?" she asked him. "No," he replied, "I am waiting for a friend. He is to come and see me at half-past seven. You can serve our dinner in a quarter of an hour. He will probably be here in a few minutes and he will certainly be hungry."

Louis took out the letter that Charles had written to him, and read it again. Would he really come tonight? He wondered why Charles had chosen this hotel so far from the town. Then, as he was putting back the letter into his pocket, the door opened and Charles appeared.

XVII

The doctor turned round sharply and looked at the house. There was no sign of life; the shutters were still closed.

"Who is there, and what do you want?" he shouted. At first nobody answered, but at the end of a few moments he heard the cry once more. He tried to open the door, but it was locked.

Instead of continuing his walk, he decided to retrace his steps. He was sure some misfortune had happened.
10 The mayor and priest knew all the inhabitants of the village. They would be able to help him. One of them would give him the necessary information.

Fortunately the mayor was at home. He listened attentively to the doctor's story and said: "It's no doubt
15 Madame Ponson's house. She has been living there for thirty years. She is at least seventy. She has only one servant, who is almost as old as herself. I will come with you at once."

XVIII

"What has happened?" asked the girl.

Hearing her voice for the second time, Luis realized who she was: one of his sister's friends. Clearly she did not remember him, after so many years.

5 "I don't know," he replied. "The lift has stopped between two floors, but don't be afraid. I don't think there is any danger. We shall have to wait for a while."

"But I shall be late at the office, and I don't like that."

Luis could not help laughing. "Miss Velez, . . ."
10 he began.

"You know me?" she cried in surprise. "Who are you?"

Then Luis had an idea; he would give a false name, and amuse himself in this way for half an hour. He told
15 her that his name was Damaso Jelez, and asked her a lot of questions about his former companions. Then he said innocently, "And what do you think of Luis Martin?"

XIX

Last week John and Frank made an excursion into the country. They got up very early, in order to be at the station at eight o'clock. When John left the house the air was cool and the sky was covered with clouds. Frank, who lives in the next street, was waiting at the 5 corner. They ran to the station as quickly as they could. On the train they met some friends and sang songs with them.

At a small village they got out and walked to a big field; here they sat down in the shade of a big oak-tree 10 and had their lunch. The sun now broke through the clouds and shone brightly on the fields and woods. In the afternoon they bathed in the nearby lake; the water was warm and both boys were good swimmers.

XX

I wondered why the letter from Genoa should make my father worry. He received dozens of letters every week, but he had never before been afraid to open one. There must be something strange about this one.

He went on turning it over and over in his hand. At 5 last he decided to open it. He took from the envelope a sheet of paper, which he unfolded and read. Silently he put it down on the table, took off his glasses and put them on top of it. Then suddenly he picked up the letter again and gave it to my mother. While she was 10 reading it, he struck the table with his hand. When my mother had finished, her face was red.

I could not guess why my parents were so angry, until they showed me the letter. When I had read it, I understood. 15

21

XXI

Vidal did not know what to do. "Where can the janitor be?" he wondered. "It is strange that he is not at home. I must find him. He will need the keys tomorrow morning, and I don't want to have to come
5 here again so early."

He walked slowly along the pavement and looked at his watch. It was 9.15. He remembered there was a telephone in the Library, and decided to ring his wife to let her know he would be late.

10 Turning round, he went towards the large door, opened it, and entered the dark, silent hall. Knowing the building well, he was able to find his way easily. Suddenly he heard footsteps behind him. "Do not move," said a voice. "What are you doing here?"

XXII

Everything was now quite ready. Jack put in his pocket the beautiful watch which his grandmother had given him. Of course he did not want to leave his little bedroom, for he had spent many happy days there in
5 the last years.

"I don't know what I shall do," he thought. "Perhaps I can find work in a large town or on a farm. I am strong, and have often worked all day without getting tired." Once again he looked out of the window.

10 On the other side of the street he saw the roof of the big house, where his great friend Harry lived with his parents. But Harry could not come with him. He opened the door and crept downstairs, as the church clock was striking two.

XXIII

It was Friday evening. As his parents had gone to the theatre, Jim was spending the evening alone. "I can do my homework on Sunday," he thought, and opened a detective story which he took from the table.

It was ten o'clock when he went into the kitchen in 5 order to fetch a piece of cake and a glass of milk. A few minutes later he was again sitting in the dining-room with his book, when he heard a car in the street.

Before he could drink his milk someone knocked. He put down the glass and hurried to the front door. There 10 was nobody there, but in the light of the moon he could see a man lying in the middle of the road.

XXIV

The same mysterious noise was heard the next night. Although they had all gone to bed early, they could not go to sleep; they were afraid and lay awake, waiting for the noise. In the morning a score of men took their guns and walked along the embankment of the river, 5 firing at every shadow which moved. They found nothing, however, and that night the noise began again.

It was obvious that, since the howls were only heard by night, it was useless to try to do anything by day; 10 but no one was willing to go to the river after sunset. At last, however, Riccardo and his friend, Giuseppe, decided to meet at nine o'clock and walk down to the river together. They arrived, trembling with fear, and hid behind a tree under the embankment. The hours 15 passed; everything grew silent; the moon rose.

XXV

I walked on. Every few hundred yards I came to a
square. All the streets and squares were exactly alike.
Everywhere there were little houses with their doors,
windows and shutters closed. Everything was white
5 and glittered in the sunshine. There was no one to be
seen. Sometimes I thought I could hear a whisper behind the shutters; once or twice I had the impression
that someone was looking out at me suspiciously.

Suddenly I felt afraid. What sort of town had I come
10 to, I wondered, and why was it deserted? I stopped
and made up my mind to return to the station and escape
as soon as I could. Then I realized that I was lost and
should have to ask someone the way. I should have to
knock at one of the houses until someone opened the
15 door. I chose the nearest one.

XXVI

Father Joseph had been living in Canada for several
years, and knew at what prices furs could be sold in the
big towns. "Show them to me, Samson," he exclaimed.
He examined them very carefully, and perceived at
5 once that they were of excellent quality. "I will try to
find you a purchaser," he said.

The news spread rapidly; everyone liked the old
man and it was thought that he knew an Englishman
who would pay prices much higher than those of
10 Bessette. A few days later, more than thirty trappers
had offered their finest skins to Father Joseph.

As he was not able to take them all, he took Samson's
best furs and left the others at a friend's house. Then he
went on foot to a small town, where there was a rail-
15 way station. There he sold some of the furs, and with
the money he received he bought a ticket to Toronto.

XXVII

There were two small windows; fortunately for us, they were protected by closed shutters. The hut was about five metres long and four metres wide. There was a bench against one wall, and in one corner we saw a heap of wood which seemed to be fairly dry.

Our faithful servant lit a fire in the middle of the hut. There was no chimney; the smoke escaped by a hole in the roof. Soon we were all sitting round the fire, except the maid who was lying on the bench; Rosko had wrapped her in his overcoat.

The wolves were still howling and throwing themselves against the door. Some tried even to jump on to the roof. We hoped they would go away before sunrise. We had no longer any horses, however, and the women would not be able to walk very far.

XXVIII

My father told my schoolmaster, who called to me one day: "Now, Luciano, I want you to count from one to a hundred." I wondered if he were mad. However, I went out in front of the class, and counted up to sixteen easily. But then I could remember only a few numbers, and so I went on: "Twenty-two, fifty-four, ninety-eight." "Stop," said the master. "Begin again." I began again but still did not succeed in counting beyond sixteen without a mistake. "Where were you when your friends were learning to count?" roared the master. "On my feet," I said. But though this answer was true, it made him very angry. He sent me home with a note to my father, asking him to punish me. I left the school and set out on my way home; I was afraid my parents would be furious with me.

XXIX

After about ten minutes we heard the station-master's whistle. The passengers began to board the train, and we knew we were about to leave. Don Alberto put his head out of the window and looked
5 anxiously along the platform, but could see no sign of our fellow-traveller. He called to a porter, "I say! Look if there is a gentleman in the buffet. He is going to miss the train." The porter merely shook his head, knowing it was too late to do anything. As the train was
10 drawing out, poor Don Alberto dropped disconsolately into his seat. Suddenly a thought occurred to me. I turned round and saw on the seat . . . a suitcase, a hat and a coat! "It doesn't matter so much that he has missed the train," I said. "He can catch another, after
15 all. But what are we going to do with his luggage?"

XXX

For many of my friends the project was still rather vague. They listened to Pierre's stories and that was all. But I was already sixteen years old; I was no longer a child, and I wanted to go at once. Besides, I
5 did not like the life I led at school. Why shouldn't I see the world?

One evening my father received my terminal marks. I had not worked well and they were very bad. My father became angry; he said I was lazy and that he
10 would punish me. I ran out of the house and went to the place on the beach where we used to meet Pierre every afternoon.

I looked at the sea, which was calm that evening. I should have liked to see a ship pass by, but there was
15 none. In two days I should have to go back to Rennes. Suddenly I heard Pierre's voice. "What is the matter, Louis?" he asked. "You look sad this evening."

26

XXXI

It was still dark when we got up. We dressed quickly, crept out of the big room where the other boys were sleeping, and were soon outside. Today was the last day of the holidays, the evening train would take us home and we hoped to spend a long day in the 5 mountains.

It was a beautiful summer morning, but the air was quite cool, as the sun was still behind the trees. We decided to walk for two hours before we had breakfast, so we hurried through the meadows and began to climb. 10

After some time we came out of the forest. "I'm hungry," I said, "why can't we stop here by the stream?" Without answering Harry placed his knapsack on the ground, and we were soon eating the sausage and bread we had brought with us. 15

XXXII

The grandmother knew very well the dangers of the sea. Her husband had been drowned many years before, and she had lived in poverty, bringing up her children as best she could. But the father insisted, and Pascualet was most pleased. 5

The following week the boats were ready, and the fishermen prepared to leave. One evening they went down to the beach, accompanied by their families, and said good-bye.

Pascualet was very happy on his first voyage. The 10 weather was good, and although he had to work hard he enjoyed the open-air life. He thought proudly that he was earning his living at his father's side. When they returned to the little port with their boat laden with fish of all kinds, they laughed at the grandmother's 15 fear. She only looked at Pascualet sadly and kept on saying, "We'll see."

XXXIII

This is how my uncle Aristide had been taken prisoner. He had gone for a walk in the forest one day. He set out early in the morning. Having walked for several hours, he suddenly realized that he was lost,
5 and that he did not know how to find his way back to the town. He was tired and hungry, and sat down to rest; he soon fell asleep. When he awoke, it was nearly dark, and he was surrounded by redskins. They bound his hands and led him away to their village.
10 At first he thought it would be impossible to escape. Then, however, when he heard them say that no white man could handle a bow, an idea came to him. He made signs to them, asking to be given a bow. When they understood what he wanted, they laughed, and gave
15 him their biggest bow.

XXXIV

Next morning, Mariette's mother was still very ill. When he heard this news, Jacques exclaimed: "Mariette, I am going down to Sallanches."

"You are mad," she replied. "With this weather, it
5 is impossible."

"There is no doctor here; I must go. I'll find your father and explain to him what has happened; and I'll ask Doctor Montiez to come back with me."

"You will never get there. I won't let you go!" said
10 Mariette.

"Listen, Mariette. Make me some hot coffee and give me something to eat."

Half an hour later, Jacques began his journey. At the end of two hours, he was so tired that he had to rest
15 for a few minutes. Then, to his great astonishment, he

saw in the distance a man and a woman dressed like Parisians.

"Do they come from the aeroplane which crashed last night?" he asked himself.

XXXV

Jack did not sleep well and woke up early. The sun was shining into his bedroom, although it was only half past six. He got up at once to waken his brother Harry, for they wanted to leave the house soon after breakfast.

When Jack pulled him out of bed, Harry got very 5 angry and cried, "What are you doing? Can't you let me sleep?" "Don't be an ass," answered Jack. "Have you forgotten that today is Tuesday? We must hurry, or we shall miss the train."

The boys dressed and went down into the kitchen, 10 where their mother had prepared all kinds of things for the journey. After a few minutes father came in from the garden and they all sat down at the table without waiting.

XXXVI

On the evening before Christmas a small boy was wandering through the dense forest, where the snow lay deep on the ground. It was terribly cold and he was very hungry, for he had eaten nothing since the breakfast which a friendly old lady had given him. Now he 5 was looking for a house where he could sleep. He had no money and was quite alone in the world. His father and mother died when he was quite young, and now he was hoping to find work in order to earn money.

Suddenly in the distance he heard children singing a 10 Christmas carol and then he saw a light in a little house.

He hurried towards the house and knocked. The door was quickly opened and soon he was sitting with the children before a large fire.

XXXVII

Hoping that the maid was still near, I began to call. There was no reply. I shouted as loudly as I could, "Help! Help! Open the door!" Still there was silence, and I became increasingly desperate. I shrieked like a
5 mad woman. Then, realizing that all this was useless, I took off my coat, my Parisian hat and my elegant gloves, and began to bang violently against the door. It would not yield. The minutes passed. I looked at my watch. It was already five minutes to eight, and
10 the reception was to have started punctually at eight. Everybody would be anxious because of my absence. This was my first meeting with my fiancé's family, and I wanted to make a good impression.

Then, suddenly, I heard a bell ringing in the distance.
15 The sound grew louder, and then I knew that it was the bell of the fire brigade.

XXXVIII

Giuseppe had lived here as a boy. In those days his family had been rich. But his father had been a man of strange habits, and instead of depositing his money in the bank, he used to keep it at home in a box, which he
5 used to hide in a secret place.

One day Giuseppe, returning from school, had found his mother in tears and his brothers running hither and thither in a state of despair. The box was no longer in its accustomed place. The money had vanished!
10 With the little money that remained to him Giuseppe's

father had bought a cottage for the family. But in spite
of his poverty he had refused to sell the old house.
For twenty years it had remained empty.

Now Giuseppe had returned, and the spirit of the
house was still there. A thought struck him. Perhaps 15
the spirit could tell him what had happened that day,
twenty years ago, when the money had disappeared.

XXXIX

Before long, I obtained complete liberty to go where-
ever I wished. Sometimes the three of us did not
attend school, but we went down to the sea instead and
spent the day there. Don Hilario, our master, sent
word to my mother that we had not been seen in his 5
school on those occasions; but as I was growing up
strong and tall, she always treated the matter lightly.

On Sundays and school holidays, we were not content
to remain down by the harbour. We climbed to the top
of the rocks and went into the caves, where we often 10
lost our way. When at last we came out, it was getting
dark and we were tired, hungry and thirsty; but we had
enjoyed ourselves.

An old fisherman, who could tell the most extra-
ordinary yarns, said to us:— 15

"One fine day, the big serpent with wings, will
suddenly come across you; and then you'll wish you
had not disobeyed your schoolmaster."

But we all laughed!

XL

As the crocodile did not show itself that day, I went
home and forgot about it.

A few days later, however, I had to make a journey.

It was necessary to cross that same river, and when I
5 reached it, I tried to make my horse enter the water.
He did so unwillingly, and as soon as he had entered it,
he stopped. The river was very narrow, and I should
have liked to swim across it, but I could not leave my
horse. I tried to push him into the water, but he jumped
10 backwards and refused to move. Then for the first time
I noticed that there was a crocodile on the bank, close
to us. It was six metres long, and was standing with
its tail in the water, as if it were about to bathe and
wanted to be sure that the water was not too cold.

SECTION II

ADVANCED LEVEL

XLI

(*a*) One summer night, a few months after my marriage, I was seated by my own hearth smoking a last pipe and nodding over a novel. My wife had already gone upstairs, and the sound of the locking of the hall door some time before told me that the servants 5 had also retired. I had risen from my seat and was knocking out the ashes of my pipe, when I suddenly heard the clang of the bell.

I looked at the clock. It was a quarter to twelve. This could not be a visitor at so late an hour. A patient, 10 evidently, and possibly an all-night sitting. With a wry face I went out into the hall and opened the door. To my astonishment, it was Sherlock Holmes who stood upon my step.

"Ah, Watson," said he, "I hoped that I might not 15 be too late to catch you."

"My dear fellow, pray come in."

I was well aware that nothing but business of importance could have brought him to me at such an hour.

(*b*) Seeing that a man such as his brother had des- 20 cribed had come out, carrying as much jewellery as he could, John called a policeman. They both ran after him. As a boy, John had run faster than any of his friends, but now, however fast he ran, he could not run fast enough to catch up with the thief. When the 25

policeman had succeeded in catching him, he asked him
why he had entered the house. Weeping with shame,
the latter replied that he had done so, not because he
wanted riches, but because his children were hungry.

XLII

(*a*) I did not mention, before Cullum left, the time
of the train by which we should start in the morning,
and while we were travelling to London I kept wishing
that I had done so. But when we reached Victoria, he
5 was waiting on the platform. He came up to us with a
rather shy smile, and explained that he had reckoned
on this train being our best connection. He gave me
flowers, so much less sensible, so far more precious than
the chocolate which the practical Gerald had provided.
10 We were very thankful for the chocolate before the
journey was over, but Cullum's roses were in the way
all the time until they were left behind accidentally at
Dieppe. I was really sorry when I found they were
gone; I loved their charming unsuitability; they were
15 typically his gift.

(*b*) If I had not been ill, I should have gone there.
He died not on March 16th, but on July 17th.
They were not allowed to enter the room without
taking off their wet shoes.
20 Her younger brother had been living in Berlin for
several months.
I promised his poor mother to give it to him the next
morning.

XLIII

(*a*) In all professions there must be competition, and
where there is competition there must be jealousy.

This passion is certainly as prevalent in the military profession as in any other. The reason may be that it is a profession in which opportunity of proving talent 5 comes so seldom, that those who believe that they possess it may never receive the wholesome correction afforded by experience. Politicians and lawyers are making speeches all the time, and it is soon shown who can make the better one. The same is true of writers, 10 musicians, painters and actors. But those who are employed in the fighting services can only show their true quality in war-time, and wars, though all too frequent, are not perpetual. Even in war the element of luck is ever present. When a brave soldier, having done his 15 duty, finds himself neglected in favour of another, who has seen less fighting, but has been more fortunate, and whom he deems his inferior in every way, the bitterness that creeps into his heart is very terrible.

(b) Having finished his affairs of State, the king had 20 gone up into his study, where, believing himself to be poorer than he was, he was counting his money. The queen, his wife, was in the dining-room, where, for some hours, she had been eating bread and honey, which she had had prepared for her. The maid, as soon as 25 she had washed the clothes, had put them out to dry in the garden. But as she was returning, thinking that all was well, a large bird attacked her and removed her nose.

XLIV

A quarter of an hour's walk took them to Signor Polani's residence. They rang twice at the main entrance before a face appeared at the little window in the door and asked who was there.

5   "I wish to see Signor Polani at once," Francis said.
"The signor went to bed an hour ago," the man said.
"Never mind that," Francis replied. "I am Francis
Hammond, and I have important news to give him."
As soon as the servant recognized Francis' voice he
10 opened the door.

"Have you news of the ladies?" he asked eagerly. "I
have news which will, I hope, lead to something,"
Francis replied.

A moment later the voice of Polani himself, who had
15 not yet gone to sleep, was heard at the top of the great
stairs, inquiring who it was who had come so late, for
although men had been arriving all day with reports
from the various islands and villages, he thought that
no one would come at this hour unless his news were
20 important. Francis at once answered.

"It is I, Signor Polani, Francis Hammond. I have
news which I think may be of importance, but I may be
mistaken."

XLV

(a) When *Ivanhoe* was produced, the carpenters
eagerly seized their opportunity. Great quantities of
timber had been ordered, for in those days everything
had to look as real as possible. There were so many
5 buildings, fences, trees, rivers and animals on the stage
that there was hardly room for the unlucky singers; it
was evident that if something were not done they would
have to sing in the adjoining market. I waited until the
final rehearsal. The burning of the castle was certainly
10 an astonishing success, but it was little admired by the
performers on the crowded stage. For regardless of the
value of human life, huge chunks of wood flew in every

direction, spreading terror among attackers and defenders alike. There was almost a riot, and undoubtedly there would have been no performance at all if I had 15 not given my word to control the zeal of the realists.

(b) The soldier was given his ticket as he was about to leave the station.

After having sold his house, he lived with an acquaintance, a schoolmaster. 20

He ought not to have come here without visiting his mother.

He knows that because he is not rich, he cannot buy the book.

I shall wait for the Germans. They will not arrive 25 until tomorrow.

XLVI

(a) We dismounted and were shown into a large room where the magistrate sat at a table on which lay a great number of papers. He was a thin-faced old man with stiff grey whiskers like a cat's. Scarcely had we all entered when a hen, leading her family of a dozen 5 chickens, rushed into the room. The chickens dispersed in search of crumbs, while the mother, more ambitious, perched on the table, tossing the papers right and left.

"Devil take the fowls," cried the magistrate, getting up in a fury. "Antonio, go and fetch your mistress this 10 very instant." The servant went out and returned after two or three minutes, followed by a fat woman who sat down, quite exhausted, on a bench. "What's the matter, Fernando?" she asked, with an amiable smile. "How dare you ask me such a question?" bawled the magis- 15 trate. "Take your fowls away before I have them all killed."

While his wife calmly moved forward, he began to
hurl books and rulers at the unfortunate birds, and at
20 last they were all driven out. A sentinel stood on guard
at the door, with orders to decapitate the first chicken
that attempted to approach.

(*b*) I am expecting to have to work late, so don't
wait too long for me.
25 You shouldn't have told him about it. Perhaps he
would never have known.

Do you remember my old uncle, the one who used to
spend so many hours working in our garden?

There has been too much rain lately, hasn't there?
30 If only the sun would shine for a few days!

As soon as it gets cooler we intend to go as far as the
nearest village and post our letters.

XLVII

(*a*) Arthur was approaching the village when, at a
turning in the road, he saw a figure in front of him
which it was impossible to mistake for anyone else than
Adam, even if there had been no grey, tailless dog at his
5 heels. He was walking at his usual rapid pace and
Arthur pushed on his horse to overtake him, for he
retained too much of his boyish feeling for Adam to
miss an opportunity of chatting with him. I will not say
that his love for that good fellow did not owe some of
10 its force to the love of patronage; our friend Arthur
liked to do everything that was handsome and to have
his handsome deeds recognised. Adam looked round
as he heard the sound of the horse's hoofs and waited
for the horseman. He would have done more for Arthur
15 than for any other young man in the world.

(*b*) A friend of mine told me that you were living in the neighbourhood. How long have you been here?

I expect you will find much to interest you.

There are some churches which are said to be worth seeing and within easy reach on a bicycle.   20

If you are not too busy, I hope we shall see one another from time to time.

I am almost always at home in the evening, so don't forget to pay me a visit.

XLVIII

(*a*) I had begun to like Ernest. I don't know why, but I have never heard that any young friend of mine was going to get married without hating his intended, though I had never seen her. I have observed that most bachelors feel the same thing, though we are generally   5 at some pains to hide the fact. That a young man of such promise should fling himself away upon such a person as Ellen was quite too provoking, and the more so because of the unexpectedness of the whole affair.

I begged him not to marry Ellen yet—not, at least,   10 until he had known her for a longer time—but he would not hear of it. I had hitherto found him upon most matters singularly easy to manage, but on this point I could do nothing with him. I would have told him of his true position, but I knew very well that this would   15 only make him more bent on having his own way—for with so much money, why should he not please himself?

(*b*) I was sorry to miss you the other day when you were passing through London.

Unfortunately, I had an engagement which I was   20 unable to avoid.

The worst of it is that I do not know when I shall have the chance of seeing you again.

Don't allow yourself to be overcome by the difficulty
25 of the job you have undertaken.

As soon as you have learned your duties, let me
know if there is any way in which I can help you.

XLIX

(*a*) The fiddle came down with him in the morning
when he rose, and during the day might be found anywhere at all. It was a miracle that it escaped being
thrown on to the fire, or stamped to pieces under the
5 children's feet. There were occasional terrible moments
when it really disappeared, and nobody would help him
in the search. Once it was away from him for a whole
night, and he sat on his bed in the dawn, and was wholly
uncomforted by his magic tree. But he did not believe
10 that it was lost, and he was right, for during the morning
a neighbour brought it timidly to the door. He learned
to be careful, however, after that, and seldom let the
fiddle out of his hands.

But now Marget announced boldly that she meant
15 to destroy it before she was done. Perhaps she was
really ashamed because her father-in-law had fiddled in
the street; she had so little of any other shame that at
least there was plenty to spare.

(*b*) When Mary had been in Florence for a week,
20 her hostess, Signora Neri, allowed her to go shopping
for the first time. She went and bought some fruit and
vegetables, and in less than half an hour she had finished.
As soon as she had finished, she hurried home with her
basket. She was glad that she had been able to help
25 Signora Neri. In three days Mary has to go home. As
soon as she arrives she will make her father write a
letter to Signora Neri, thanking her for all she has done
for his daughter.

L

(*a*) There was an old tramp in my native town who used to sit for hours on the shady side of a ruined barn, and with his home-made whistle to his lips, and tapping one foot on the ground, he produced the most wonderful melodies. At length, I made a whistle exactly like 5 his and diligently practised such songs as I knew. I must have annoyed my relations greatly, for when my father saw me about to play, he would instantly set me some useful task. And at the sight of my stern aunt I always secreted my whistle in my coat-pocket 10 and escaped to the attic, like a cat caught stealing the cream.

(*b*) Anne decided that she must see Richard at once. But since the day was so fine, she was tempted to see Cologne instead. The morning was spent happily in 15 looking into the windows of the shops and in buying herself an umbrella; afterwards she lunched alone, thinking that it would be better to arrive at Richard's house in the afternoon. "I can never get lost so long as I can find the river," she said to herself, "for if I follow 20 it I cannot fail to find the bridge." She did not find it, however, until about three o'clock, and when at last she had mounted the staircase and knocked at the door, she was prepared for him to be out.

LI

(*a*) One day as Daffy and Maggie returned together from the village across the river, she, impatiently urging him to hurry, stumbled against him from the rear. Down he went into deep water, and, borne along by the swift current, did not again reach surface till he found 5

himself in the dark, dangerous whirlpool below the big rock. Maggie was then screaming aloud for help; he shouted to reassure her, and immediately the screams stopped. When he rejoined her she begged him to
10 forgive her, though she still declared that it was his fault. He promised to conceal the episode from even his uncle.

(*b*) Since I had arrived at the airport in a government car I was received with some ceremony. I ought,
15 I suppose, to have celebrated my first flight by being extremely excited, but instead I went sound asleep. The next thing I knew was that I was being woken by an official (who was evidently displeased by my apparent lack of interest) with a special invitation to visit
20 the pilot. I found it very difficult to reach him, as I had to crawl through a narrow passage where luggage was stacked. On account of the deafening noise no conversation was possible. Night had fallen, but the moon was lighting up the fleecy white clouds over which we
25 were flying. I stood fascinated, until the pilot politely told me to go back to my seat.

LII

(*a*) When I awoke again it was day. Everything was quite still, and I could see nothing on the road. I crawled out of the ditch and set off again. I walked several hours, and then I met a boy on a bicycle riding
5 from the direction from which I had come. He stared at me and stopped when I spoke to him. I asked him to tell me the way to Chalford. He said that it was more than thirty miles away in the direction I had come. I thanked him and continued on my way.

I don't know how long I was on the road. I remem- 10
ber stopping to sleep now and then, sometimes in the
day-time and sometimes at night, and I remember that
several people gave me food, and one woman once gave
me a cup of milk which did me good. I remember
nothing clearly though, except that after I seemed to 15
have been walking for weeks I saw houses which I
recognized as Chalford. There were women sitting at
the doors of the cottages but I was a little stronger now
and I hurried on to reach home.

(*b*) "But what are we going to do?" I asked him, 20
hiding my trembling hands behind my back and trying
not to reveal either to him or to anyone else how it had
all frightened me. "We would never have got lost if
we had done what the other two advised. We ought to
have listened to them, Joe." 25

"Shut up," Joe replied. "What's the use of talking
about it? We have got to act!"

LIII

(*a*) The house in the Rue St. Honoré had two doors
that opened upon the street, the one from the shop and
the other from the room we called the parlour, in which
we had our meals. We had an old servant, who was in
the service of my grandfather for over forty years, but 5
she never slept in the house; and it was our habit to
get our own supper in the evenings, when the old man
and I would talk for an hour or so before we went to
bed.

And thus we were sitting in the parlour at about nine 10

o'clock on the evening of the 13th of July, when I heard a noise in the distance that sounded to me like the beating of drums and the shouting of many people.

"What's that?" I exclaimed, springing to my feet—
15 for it was a kind of angry noise that I had heard. Naturally my grandfather had heard nothing, for he was fairly deaf, but as we listened, the noise came nearer and nearer, and when he, too, had risen from his chair, he was quicker than I to realize what it meant.

20 (*b*) I don't remember my grandmother's age. She must be over eighty. But it seems to me she has never grown old. She may be grey-haired, and recently her health has been less good. But what kindness! What charm! What lovely bright eyes! It is quite obvious
25 that everyone is devoted to her. My sister and I would do anything to please her.

LIV

(*a*) The family sitting-room was a long room with a window at each end; one looking along the banks of the river, the other into the mill yard. Maggie was sitting with her work against the latter window when she saw
5 Mr. Wakem entering the yard, as usual, on his fine horse, but this time not alone. Someone was with him, a figure in a cloak. Maggie had hardly time to feel that it was Philip come back, before they were in front of the window and he was raising his hat to her; while his
10 father, catching the movement by a side glance, looked sharply at them both.

Maggie hurried away and carried her work upstairs; she felt that the meeting with Philip would be robbed of all its pleasure in the presence of the two fathers.
15 Some day, perhaps, she could see him when they could

just shake hands, and she could tell him that she remembered his goodness to Tom, and the things he had said to her in the old days, though they could never be friends any more.

(*b*) I don't think you are right in saying that he was 20 in Spain three years ago. I am sure that it was the year before that; for I intended to go then on business and I should have gone with him, only that I got ill and when I recovered I could not get a seat in the plane. So he went off before I could start. In the end it proved 25 impossible for me to get away at all. I am not altogether sorry, as at that time things were not nearly so easy for travellers as they are now.

LV

(*a*) When the first Europeans at last ventured to cross this greatest of all oceans, they discovered to their amazement that right out in the midst of it lay a number of small mountainous islands and flat coral reefs isolated from each other and from the world in general by vast 5 areas of sea. And every single one of these islands was already inhabited by people who had come there before them—tall, handsome people who met them on the beach with dogs and pigs and fowls. They talked a language which no other people knew. And the men of 10 our race, who boldly called themselves the discoverers of the islands, found cultivated fields, and villages with temples and huts, on every single habitable island. On some, indeed, they found old pyramids, paved roads, and carved stone statues as high as a four-storey house 15 in Europe. But the explanation of the whole mystery was lacking. Who were these people and where had they come from?

(*b*) When I lived in the country I used to go to
20 London three times a week, but for a while after the
war I went only once, and now my visits are few and far
between. Not that I don't like London; on the contrary,
there is always something going on which is worth
seeing. But as I get older I find the journey more and
25 more tiring, so that I don't really enjoy the theatre, or
whatever it is that takes me there. Besides, nowadays,
there is such a crowd and everybody seems to be
hurrying about at top speed.

LVI

(*a*) I came across America, visiting Brigham Young
on the way. I did not achieve great intimacy with the
great leader. I called upon him, sending to him my
card, apologizing for doing so without an introduction,
5 and excusing myself by saying that I did not like to pass
through the territory without seeing a man of whom I
had heard so much. He received me in his doorway,
not asking me to enter, and inquired whether I were not
a miner. When I told him I was not a miner, he asked
10 me whether I earned my bread. I told him that I did.
"I guess you are a miner," said he. I again assured him
that I was not. "Then how do you earn your bread?"
I told him that I did so by writing books. "I'm sure
you are a miner," said he. Then he turned upon his
15 heel, went back into the house, and closed the door. I
was properly punished, as I was vain enough to con-
ceive that he would have heard my name.

(*b*) Yesterday was one of the most interesting days
I have ever spent. My aunt, whose favourite niece I
20 am, visited us, which was a pleasant surprise. I was

46

glad she came yesterday, because if she had come any other day, I should have been at school. We had a walk in the country, and saw hundreds of beautiful flowers. In the evening she took me to the theatre. I think actresses must have an interesting life. They are talked 25 of and admired and given handsome gifts, and I should like to be one when I grow up.

LVII

(*a*) Among the inmates at Secheron, on his arrival at Geneva, Lord Byron had found Mr. and Mrs. Shelley, and a female relative of the latter, who had about a fortnight before taken up their residence at this hotel. It was the first time that Lord Byron and Mr. Shelley 5 ever met; though, long before, when the latter was quite a youth—being the younger of the two by four or five years—he had sent to the noble poet a copy of his first poem, accompanied by a letter in which, after de-tailing at full length all the accusations he had heard 10 brought against his character, he added, that, should these charges not have been true, it would have made him happy to be honoured with his acquaintance. The book alone, it appears, reached its destination—the letter having miscarried—and Lord Byron was known 15 to have expressed warm admiration of the opening lines of the poem.

On their present meeting at Geneva, therefore, an intimacy almost immediately sprang up between them.

(*b*) "That must be three o'clock," thought John, 20 hearing the clock strike. "It is strange my parents are not here yet. However long the journey is, they should have arrived by now." As soon as the clock had finished

striking, he went out to learn what had happened. Out-
25 side he met his cousin Mary. Taking off his hat like the
courteous young man he was, he asked her for news.
Neither his father nor hers, he learned, would be able
to leave Venice till the following week. She ended by
inviting him to dinner.

LVIII

(*a*) My principal object in these excursions was the
pleasure of seeing romantic scenery, or what afforded
me at least equal pleasure, the places which had been
distinguished by remarkable historical events. The
5 delight with which I regarded the former, of course,
had general approbation, but I often found it difficult
to procure sympathy with the interest I felt in the latter.
Yet to me the wandering over the field of Bannockburn
was the source of more exquisite pleasure than gazing
10 upon the celebrated landscape from the towers of Stir-
ling Castle. Show me an old castle or a field of battle,
and I was at home at once, filled it with its combatants
in their proper costume, and overwhelmed my hearers
by the enthusiasm of my description. In crossing Magus
15 Moor, near St. Andrews, the spirit moved me to give a
picture of the assassination of the Archbishop of St.
Andrews to some fellow-travellers, and one of them,
though well acquainted with the story, protested my
narrative had frightened away his night's sleep.

20 (*b*) I am glad that you are about to go to Italy.
Travelling is a great pleasure, but what a pity one has
to leave one's friends behind. I am sorry, too, that one
cannot get to the continent without crossing the sea.

I hope the weather will be better than when I went to France last year. If the sea is rough, the crossing will 25 seem far longer than it really is.

Take a camera with you, so that you will be able to take photographs of the buildings you like. In Italy you will see many fine sights.

LIX

(a) Our conversation drew to its close and I got up to say good-bye. Stalin seemed suddenly embarrassed and said in a more cordial tone: "You are leaving at daybreak. Why should we not go to my house and have some drinks?" He led the way through many 5 passages and rooms till we came out into a roadway still within the Kremlin, and in a couple of hundred yards gained his apartment. He showed me his own rooms which were of moderate size, simple, dignified and four in number—dining-room, working-room, bed- 10 room and a large bathroom. Presently there appeared first a very aged house-keeper and later a handsome red-haired girl who kissed her father dutifully.

Winston Churchill

(b) When he got to the top of the wood, with only a short field to cross, the light in Adam's cottage could 15 be seen. Old Adam, a most peculiar figure, peculiar at any time, but less peculiar than usual at this hour of pre-dawn darkness when all life was subject to distortion, came out of his cottage at the sound of Geoff's approach. He carried a spade, an unlit lantern, a crow- 20 bar and a sack. The sack was unnecessary, but he said he always carried it, for there was always the chance

that something would be found to put into it. Neither
of them spoke. In silence they walked back down the
25 track by which Geoff had come.

Robert Henriques

LX

(*a*) Long ago on a Saturday night a bridal couple
with their friends feasted and danced merrily until the
hour of midnight, when the piper, who was a pious man,
refused to play any longer. This made the bride, who
5 was fond of dancing, very angry, and she swore that
she would not have her pleasure spoilt by a piper, but
would find someone to play if she went to hell to fetch
him. These words had hardly been spoken when an old
man with a long beard appeared, sat down and began
10 to play a slow and solemn melody. The company began
to dance but soon found to their horror that the musi-
cian had now changed to his proper shape as the Evil
One.

Henry Bett

(*b*) Away in a house in the deep green country Sean
15 nodded in his chair set near to a flaming fire, for the
night was cold, and even the air of the room felt frosty.
Midnight had passed by and he was sleepy, but he
thought that if he went to bed, sleep would go, for his
mind was too tired to sink deep into it. Besides the bed
20 was far off and cold, while the spot by the fire was
seductively warm, inducing a condition of wakefulness
that was halfway towards sleep. He had extinguished
the lamp, but the brilliant flaming of the fire gave
enough light to show everything in the room resting
25 among the shadows.

Sean O'Casey

(*a*) The door was opened immediately, but I was startled by the being that confronted me, particularly by her deep voice, which demanded, "Who are you? What do you want?" The woman was huge: sitting in her low chair she had appeared just a plump country-woman; standing in the doorway she towered above me more than anything human had ever done before. Surprise tied my tongue, and she repeated her questions sharply, even angrily. I stammered a reply. "I am from the other side of the hill, and I have lost my way," I said.

The woman glared at me. "Where are you going?" she asked. Again I hesitated, for I was loath to mention my grandfather's house. I was growing afraid of it.

"Well?" she said.

"How far is it to Wyselwood?" I asked.

It was the woman's turn to pause. "What would you be doing at Aaron Tyrwhitt's?"

"He is my grandfather," I replied.

The woman scrutinised me closely and for the first time seemed to note my clothing. She spoke quite civilly.

"You are out of your way. Your path lies yonder. Do you know it at all? I have not seen your face before."

(*b*) It was a very dark night. When Mary reached home, there was nobody in. She was afraid to enter alone although she had the key and so she decided to go round to Jeanne's house. She knocked on the door but there was no answer. As she had just left her friend, she wondered what had become of her. On arriving back home, she found Jeanne waiting for her there. Why hadn't they met on the way?

(*a*) My grandfather took off his spectacles and began to clean them. Perhaps he did this to hide his alarm, for I could see that his fingers were trembling.

"There are hundreds of them!" he said. "Hundreds.
5 And when people are mad like that they don't care what they do. It is hunger that has made them mad. Things, my boy, have gone too far! Much too far!" And he went on repeating that phrase, over and over again, mumbling as if to himself and still shaking his
10 head.

I went to the two doors, to make sure they were both locked; and no sooner had I done that than the old man blew out the lamp.

"They must think we have gone to bed," said he.
15 "I am going up to my bedroom, André, to see if I can find out who they are and what they want. It may be that they will pass by and take no notice of us; but I fear that that may not be so."

I had followed him into the shop; and then it was
20 that I felt frightened for the first time, for I could hear the voices of men who were talking to each other outside.

(*b*) What a difficult child she was already, at four years old! She would refuse all that she was given to
25 eat or drink, pushing away her plate or cup. Then when everything had been taken away, she would weep bitterly demanding to be fed!

Everyone pities her father and mother, though some think they ought to have been more severe when she
30 was younger.

(*a*) There are many motives that impel us to travel, good as well as bad. Some travel to enlarge their minds, or to write a book, and the worst of travelling for such reasons is that it so often implants in the traveller, when he returns, a desire to enlarge other 5 people's minds too. Unhappily, it needs a gift of vivid description and a careful art of selection to make the story of one's travels interesting.

A friend of mine returned the other day from a journey and told me that he had received a rebuke 10 which cured him forever of recounting his experiences. He was lunching with his brother and was talking with what he thought was great brilliance, when his eldest nephew, aged eight, towards the end of the meal, laid down his spoon and fork and said piteously to his 15 mother: "Mummy, I *must* talk; it makes me so tired to hear uncle going on like that."

Perhaps, for most people, the best results of travel are that they return with a sense of grateful security to the familiar scene. It is good to be at home again. 20

(*b*) When you come to pay me a visit I hope you will stay as long as your work permits. I don't think you know this part of the country, do you? It is not one of those which attract tourists; its beauties are not, so to say, apparent at first sight. But they are, none 25 the less, there for one who has the patience to search for them. I know you are fond of taking long walks, so you can reach places which the motorist passes by without knowing that they exist, and I am sure you will thank me for having made you acquainted with 30 them.

(*a*) This point I may illustrate by a comparison between your view of the family and ours. To you English, so far as a foreigner can perceive, the family is merely a means for nourishing and protecting the
5 child until he is of age to look after himself. As early as may be, you send your boys away to a boarding school, where they quickly emancipate themselves from the influence of their home. As soon as they are of age, you send them out, as you say, to "make their fortune",
10 and from that moment, often enough, as they cease to be dependent on their parents, so they cease to recognize obligations towards them. They may go where they will, do what they will, earn and spend as they choose; and it is at their own option whether or no they
15 maintain their family ties. With you the individual is the unit, and all the units are free. No one is tied, but also no one is rooted. To remain in the position in which you were born you consider a disgrace; a man, to be a man, must venture, struggle, compete and
20 win.

(*b*) We are often told that travel broadens the mind, but I wonder if this is true. I suppose it depends on what you mean by travel. Merely to spend a short time in a country without being able to talk to the people
25 cannot be of much use. At best, it may provide a number of pleasant memories, but it is impossible that, by such means, one could form any idea of the way of life of the foreign country, and that, more than anything else, is the benefit to be got from travel, isn't it?

(*a*) Soon after the letter, the major himself made his appearance, accompanied by Morgan, his faithful valet, without whom the old gentleman could not move. When the major travelled he wore a jaunty and juvenile travelling costume; to see his back still you would have 5 taken him for one of the young fellows whose slim waist and youthful appearance Warrington was beginning to envy. It was not until the worthy man began to move, that the observer remarked that Time had weakened his ancient knees. 10

There were noblemen both of our own country and of foreign nations present that winter at Rosenbad. Major Pendennis read over the strangers' list with great gratification on the night of his arrival, was pleased to find several of his acquaintances among the great folks, 15 and would have the honour of presenting his nephew to a German grand duchess, a Russian princess, and an English marquis, before many days were over: nor was Pen by any means averse to making the acquaintance of these great personages, having a liking for polite life, 20 and all the splendours and amenities belonging to it. What would poor Helen have thought, could she have known to what kind of people her brother-in-law was presenting her son?

(*b*) I was walking through the town the other day 25 with my friend, when we happened to pass a bookshop. My friend never sees a bookshop without wanting to go inside, and whether I liked it or not, I had to go in too. I wonder if anyone loves books more than my friend. Though he likes all books, he finds German 30 literature less interesting than French or Italian.

Half an hour later, we came out of the shop with our arms full of books. I was afraid that we should never

reach home. That the Corso Cavour was the longest
35 street in the town, I had of course known before; but till
then I had never realized just how long it is.

LXVI

(*a*) We feel a natural curiosity to know what was
done and said by our forefathers, even though it may be
nothing wiser or better than what we are daily doing
or saying ourselves. Some of this generation may be
5 little aware how many conveniences, now considered to
be necessaries and matters of course, were unknown to
their grandfathers and grandmothers. In those days it
was not unusual to set men to work with shovels to fill
up holes in roads seldom used by carriages, on such
10 special occasions as a funeral or a wedding. Ignorance
and coarseness of language also were still lingering.
About this time a neighbouring squire referred the
following difficulty to Mr. Austen's decision: "You
know all about these sort of things. Do tell us. Is
15 Paris in France, or France in Paris? for my wife has
been disputing with me about it." The same gentleman,
narrating some conversation which he had heard between the vicar and his wife represented the latter as
beginning her reply to her husband with a round oath;
20 and when his daughter reminded him that Mrs. Austen
never swore, he replied: "Now, Betty, why do you pull
me up for nothing? That's neither here nor there; you
know very well that's only *my way of telling the story.*"

(*b*) When Richard had been in Paris for more than
25 three weeks, it became necessary for him to return
home in a hurry. As soon as he had packed, he drove
to the station as fast as he could. On arriving there, he

bought some books and newspapers, as well as fruit, eggs and chocolate. He then sat down in the train and tried to go to sleep, not because he was tired, but be- 30 cause he wanted to make the time pass quickly.

Although he often has journeys to make, he does not like travelling and never grows accustomed to it. However short a journey is, it is always tedious to him. He would rather have any travelling companion than travel 35 alone.

LXVII

(*a*) "Is there another way up?" asked Harriet.

"Yes, of course there is," said Miss Barton, "I ought to have thought of that. Up through the Dining Hall passage and the Library. Come along!"

"Wait a minute," said Harriet. "Whoever it is may 5 be still there. You watch the main door to see they don't get out that way. I'll go up through the Hall."

"Very well. Good idea. Here! Haven't you got a torch? You'd better take mine. You'll waste time turning on lights." 10

Harriet snatched the torch and ran, thinking hard. Miss Barton's story sounded plausible enough. She said she had woken up, seen the light (very likely she slept with her curtains drawn open) and gone out to investigate. 15

Dorothy L. Sayers

(*b*) After breakfast Augustus retired to his study to write the autobiography on which he was then engaged. He neither smoked himself, nor allowed smoking in the house, so that those of his guests who hankered for the first pipe of the day had to go out of doors, which was 20 pleasant enough in summer when you could sit down

with a book in the garden, but not so pleasant in winter when you had to seek shelter in the stables. Luncheon was at one; we were waited on by maids in black
25 uniforms, white caps and aprons and were given a substantial meal of eggs or fish, joint with vegetables, if there were no left-overs from the night before, and a sweet.

W. Somerset Maugham

LXVIII

(*a*) "Well, it's no use *your* talking about waking him," said Tweedledum, "when you're only one of the things in his dream. You know very well you're not real."

5   "I *am* real!" said Alice, and began to cry.

"You won't make yourself a bit realler by crying," Tweedledee remarked: "There's nothing to cry about."

"If I wasn't real," Alice said—half laughing through her tears, it all seemed so ridiculous—"I shouldn't be
10 able to cry."

"I hope you don't suppose those are *real* tears?" Tweedledum interrupted in a tone of great contempt.

"I know they're talking nonsense," Alice thought to herself: "and it's foolish to cry about it." So she
15 brushed away her tears, and went on, as cheerfully as she could, "at any rate I'd better be getting out of the wood."

Lewis Carroll

(*b*) She was wild to be at home—to hear, to see, to be upon the spot to share with Jane in the cares that
20 must now fall wholly upon her, and though almost persuaded that nothing could be done for Lydia, her uncle's interference seemed of the utmost importance,

58

and till he entered the room the misery of her impatience was great. Mr. and Mrs. Gardiner had hurried back in alarm, supposing by the servant's account that their 25 niece was taken suddenly ill; but satisfying them instantly in that respect, she eagerly communicated the cause of their summons and read the two letters aloud.

Jane Austen

LXIX

(*a*) He said good-bye to Annette, made his way down her stairs, and, once in the street, took off his hat and wiped his forehead. Rue Lilas. Well, he thought, it has a pretty name anyway, and set out. On the way, he bought some grapes, a bottle of red wine, a loaf of 5 bread, some sausage, and a basket to carry them in. And now, he said to himself, something quite useless; it will please her more than food and drink. Flowers? He had not hands enough to carry them, but he saw in a shop a small box with lovely flowers on its lid and 10 this he could slip into his pocket. That ought to be useless enough, Barbet thought as he marched off; and he took it out of the paper, unable to deny himself the pleasure of studying the flowers, hoping she would like them. 15

It was almost at the spot where the vegetables had fallen from the boy's cart that he emerged from the Rue La Bruyère. Rue Lilas, Number Ten, was a tall, narrow house, very dark, that smelt of onions and wet clothes. A fat child carrying a pail told him that Danielle lived 20 on the third floor, but was out.

"Out? She's not ill, then?"

"She's out," the child repeated, and off she went.

(*b*) The two girls ran back home. Their mother had
been waiting for them for more than half an hour, and
she looked worried. "What have you been doing?" she
said in a sharp tone. "What has kept you so long? You
have been gone since a quarter to five. We have been
looking for you everywhere. I am afraid your father
will be angry when he sees you covered in mud. And
look at your new dress, Mary! Just look at it! It is
torn in two places. . . You ought to have told me that
you were going to be late. Didn't anyone bring you
home?"

LXX

(*a*) Budge went back to the railway station to fetch
a box, in which both families had packed their indis-
pensable belongings. Rippingille set forth to purchase
the food. The ladies, until their luggage arrived, closely
examined each of the rooms, and tried to keep the
children quiet. Glad at not having to walk further, and
gratified by the conquest of the landlady, they were in
the mood for finding everything admirable. Impossible,
they agreed, to have done better. The place was clean;
the beds looked comfortable; they were not more than
twenty minutes' walk from the beach.

"I don't know what you think, Annie, but I call this
first-rate. Did you see the picture of the Queen and all
her family in my bedroom?"

"And look at those lovely artificial flowers! Why,
you feel you want to be smelling 'em. I don't know
what you think, but I'm going to enjoy myself!"

The first disappointment was the lateness of supper,
which, ordered for nine o'clock, was served at a quarter
to ten. The children being in bed, their parents at

length sat down to the meal with keen appetite, and soon recovered their good humour. Budge had brought in with him a bottle of wine.

(*b*) When she had finished her meal she got up quickly and walked out. On reaching the station she found that she would have to wait half an hour, as there was no train until twenty-five minutes to three.

"I should have left earlier," she thought. "I don't like people to have to wait for me. It's so rude."

She sat down in the waiting room and took a book out of her case. She had hardly begun to read when she heard footsteps approaching. She looked up and saw a man, whose face she recognized, walking along the platform. He was wearing neither hat nor coat, and looked as though he had been running.

LXXI

(*a*) Laura jumped from the cart. Beyond the gate the road turned downward and there it was at last—the grey, roughly-built house, that she vaguely remembered, with the little garden to the side and the steep hill behind. No one, apparently, had heard her coming. Was everybody at church? But it was nearly one o'clock. She knocked at the door. No answer. She knocked again, louder and louder. At last steps sounded from within and the door opened.

"I say, what are you making such a noise for?"

It was a young man, still half asleep and drawing his hand irritably across his eyes. Suddenly he perceived that the young girl standing at the door was a stranger.

"I beg your pardon, Miss, I'm sure. Did you want anything?"

The visitor laughed. "Yes, I want a good deal! I

came to see my cousins—you're one, though of course you don't remember me. I thought perhaps you'd ask me to dinner."

20 "Well, you'll have to wait till mother gets back. In the meantime, shall I put your horse in the stable? Perhaps you'd like to come in? There's a good fire and you'll want to warm yourself after driving up here."

(b) It's a long time since I heard anything of him.
25 The last news I had must have been at least a year ago, and goodness knows what may have happened in the meantime. He was always very careless about writing; that we might be anxious about him doesn't seem to him to matter, apparently. But the young are often
30 cruel without meaning to be. I shouldn't be surprised if he turned up one of these days without letting us know beforehand. It's the sort of thing I should expect him to do and I needn't say I shall be delighted to welcome him back whenever he likes to come.

LXXII

(a) When Harry was left alone, he stood by the fire thinking. He had been preparing for this moment for so long that now it was actually here he was frightened. Of course, all his thoughts had centred on his son whom
5 he had not seen since he was a baby two years old. In some unaccountable way, he had never been able to realize exactly what Robin would be. As to the others, he had never cared much for his brother in the old days. Indeed, there had been a time when he had hated him.
10 After ten years in exile the longing to see his child had grown too strong to be resisted, and he had written to his father asking for permission to return. He had

received a cold answer from his brother saying that their
father thought that, as Harry had been so successful out
there, it would be perhaps better if he remained a little 15
longer; that he would find little to do at home and
would only be bored—and so on for four closely written
pages. But that was ten years ago, and now all the past
was to be forgotten and forgiven.

(*b*) I don't know what has happened to the weather 20
lately. Who would have expected a north wind in the
middle of June? And just look at all the rain we have
had at week-ends when people want to get away from
work and get into the open air—as though it came on
purpose just to spoil the fun. As I grow older the 25
weather seems to get worse and worse.

Well, the sky has cleared for the time being, so I
think we can venture out without your having to carry a
waterproof for fear the rain may come down again.

LXXIII

(*a*) Without waiting for an answer from him, and
keeping her gaze carefully averted, the frightened
woman crept to the door and out of the room. She heard
him sit down to the table, as if to begin supper; though,
Heaven knows, his appetite was slight enough after a 5
reception which had confirmed his worst suspicion.
When Barbara had ascended the stairs and arrived in
her chamber she sank down, and buried her face in the
bedclothes.

There she remained for some time. The bed-chamber 10
was over the dining-room, and presently as she knelt,
Barbara heard Willowes thrust back his chair, and rise
to go into the hall. In five minutes that figure would

probably come up the stairs and confront her again; it
15 —this new and terrible form that was not her husband's.
In the loneliness of this night, with neither maid nor
friend beside her, she lost all self-control, and at the
first sound of his footsteps on the stairs, without so
much as flinging a cloak round her, she flew from the
20 room, ran along the gallery to the back staircase, which
she descended, and, unlocking the back door, let herself
out. She scarcely was aware what she had done till she
found herself in the garden, crouching under a bush.

(*b*) As soon as they had finished dinner, they went
25 out. The street outside was all white. "It has been
snowing," said Emily to Mary. "I hate walking in the
snow. What a pity that we have to go so far on foot.
If we had not been so lazy yesterday, we should have
been able to stay at home this evening. However, as
30 soon as my cousin's friend arrives, I shall hear what he
has to say and depart. Provided that no one detains us,
we shall be sitting by our fireside again in two hours."
"The sooner we are back the better," replied Mary.
So saying, they set out; and although walking was
35 difficult, they soon arrived.

LXXIV

(*a*) Ackroyd was staring like a man turned to stone
at a long blue envelope. The other letters he had let
drop to the ground.
"Her writing," he said in a whisper. "She must have
5 gone out and posted it last night, just before . . .
before . . . "
He ripped open the envelope and drew out a thick
enclosure. Then he looked up sharply.

64

"You're sure you shut the window?" he said.

"Quite sure," I replied, surprised. "Why?" 10

"All this evening I've had a queer feeling of being watched. What's that . . . ?"

He turned sharply. So did I. We both had the impression of hearing the latch of the door give ever so slightly. I went across and opened it. There was no- 15 one there.

Agatha Christie

(*b*) In the autumn of 1939 Hitler was well aware that the professional soldiers were opposed to extending the war by an attack in the west, particularly at the time he proposed. Hitler, however, did not abandon 20 his plans. He summoned the principal generals for another conference. Once again we are fortunate in having a report of what Hitler said. The arguments which he used were the same as those he had put forward on October 10th, but he spoke more freely. He laid 25 great stress on the fact that, for the first time since the foundation of the German Empire by Bismarck, Germany had no need to fear a war on two fronts.

Alan Bullock

LXXV

(*a*) They drove to the Savoy Hotel and lunched together in the open air underneath the glass roof. The day was very hot, the streets baked in an arid glare of sunlight; a dry dust from the wood pavement powdered those who passed by in the street outside, but here they 5 were cool and felt at their ease. He talked easily of unimportant things and pointed out from time to time some person of note or some fashionable actress who

happened to pass in or out of the hotel. He could be
10 good company when he chose, as he did on this morning.
It was not until coffee had been set before them and he
had lighted a cigar that he began to talk about themselves, and then not with any paternal tone, but rather
as one comrade conferring with another. There, indeed,
15 lay his great advantage with Sylvia. Her mother had
either disregarded her or treated her as a child. She
could not but be won by a father who laid bare his plans
to her and asked for her criticism as well as her assent.
Her suspicions of yesterday died away, or at all events
20 slept so soundly that they could not have troubled her
less had they been dead.

(*b*) Such a curious incident occurred recently right
in front of my house. A car was coming along the road
at a fair speed when suddenly one of the back wheels
25 came off and rolled away on its own account across the
road. I can't think why the car didn't fall over sideways,
but in fact it continued in a straight line until the driver
succeeded in bringing it to a stop. Meanwhile the wheel
had narrowly missed a man who happened to be walking
30 in the opposite direction. Both men are to be con-
gratulated on their good luck and I hope the owner of
the car has learned his lesson, and will see in future that
the wheels are securely fastened.

LXXVI

(*a*) Hannah shut her door that night neither at nine
nor at ten. For by the latter hour the master of the
house was still absent, and nowhere to be found, in
spite of repeated calls from the door and up the lane.
5 Hannah guessed where he had gone without much difficulty; but her guess only made her the more angry.

The children had always been troublesome—Louie more especially—but they had never done any such act of open rebellion as this before, and she was filled with a kind of silent fury as she thought of her husband going out to welcome the wanderers.

Meanwhile David and Louie, high up on the side of the mountain, were wondering with a fearful joy what might be happening at the farm. The manner of their escape had caused them much thought. Should they slip out of the front door instead of going to bed? But it was generally locked before supper by Hannah herself, and, considering how close the kitchen was to it, the children despaired of getting out unnoticed. Other plans, in which windows and ropes played a part, were discussed. David was of opinion that he alone could have managed any of them; but who'd try it with a girl?

(b) You often hear people say nowadays that the countryside is being ruined. I don't think there is much truth in this. Admittedly the main roads are terrible, especially at week-ends, but that doesn't mean that there are no quiet corners left anywhere if you take the trouble to look for them. There is always an alternative route to be found, and, even if it does take a little longer, surely it is better to drive at your ease and have a chance to look about you and admire the scenery. It may not be very imposing, but there is a quiet beauty which is very pleasing and the picturesqueness is undeniable of the many villages which still remain unspoiled.

LXXVII

(a) Oliver walked twenty miles that day; and all that time tasted nothing but the crust of dry bread, and a few draughts of water, which he begged at the cottage

doors by the roadside. When the night came, he
5 turned into a meadow; and, creeping close under a
hedge, determined to sleep there till morning. He felt
frightened at first, for the wind moaned dismally over
the empty fields, and he was cold and hungry, and more
alone than he had ever felt before. Being very tired
10 with his walk, however, he soon fell asleep and forgot
his troubles.

He felt cold and stiff when he got up next morning,
and so hungry that he was obliged to exchange his last
penny for some bread, in the very first village through
15 which he passed. He had walked no more than twelve
miles, when night closed in again. His feet were sore,
and his legs so weak that they trembled beneath him.
Another night passed in the chill damp air made him
worse; when he set forward on his journey next morn-
20 ing, he could hardly crawl along.

He waited at the bottom of a steep hill till a coach
came up, and then begged of the passengers; but there
were very few took any notice of him.

(b) The other day, we visited the village about
25 whose church you had spoken to us. Never had I seen
the trees laden with so many apples and cherries.
"There is nothing I like better than staying in the
country," said my sister. "It is you who ought to be
living here instead of me," I said to her. "I am sorry
30 we cannot live here always," she answered, "but I am
afraid we have to live in town on account of the children.
Neither good doctors nor good schools are easily found
in a little village."

I picked a flower and gave it to her, asking her
35 whether it was one she had ever seen before.

(*a*) On the whole, Tinfield got on quite well with the Americans. After all, where a man is a foreigner if he comes from a village five miles away, he isn't any more a foreigner if he comes from Kansas. The English people who didn't get on well with the G.I.s were usually those who expected the Americans to be just like themselves, and were bewildered and indignant when they were different. Tinfield never expected anything of the sort, so it had time to notice that the troops were friendly and generous, and kind to the children. I think one or two people even noticed that they were desperately lonely and homesick. So if Tinfield looked at them in its cool, slightly ironic way, and responded to most of their friendly words with "Ah" or "Mebbe", it was being friendly in its fashion.

Nigel Balchin

(*b*) Life did change for Tom and Maggie; and yet they were not wrong in believing that the thoughts and loves of these first years would always make part of their lives. We could never have loved the earth so well if we had had no childhood in it—if it were not the earth where the same flowers come up again every spring that we used to gather with our tiny fingers as we sat lisping to ourselves on the grass—the same berries in the autumn hedgerows—the same redbreasts that we used to call 'God's birds', because they did no harm to the precious crops. What novelty is worth that sweet monotony where everything is known, and *loved* because it is known?

George Eliot

(*a*) He had just time to deposit his bag in his room and have a wash before going to his appointment with Colonel Whatmore. The silk factory, which was on the outskirts of the town, occupied a good deal of ground,
5 and looked rather large and prosperous. The office occupied a central building, five storeys high; and there the Admiral gave his name to a young woman at the counter, and told her he had come to see Colonel Whatmore. After a few minutes the young woman
10 returned, looking rather worried, and said the Colonel wanted to know what he wanted. The Admiral then found the card Colonel Whatmore had given him on the previous Saturday, wrote a few words on it, and handed it over to the young woman. After another wait she
15 came back, looking downright miserable now, and conducted him along a corridor and into a small office, to confront a woman who did not smile, and seemed to regard him with mistrust. The Admiral waited for the young woman to announce him.

20 (*b*) "Which of those trees did you plant last year, Auntie?"

"Those with the small leaves. Aren't they lovely? There are some more over there. I should have liked some in that corner, but the gardener thought not. It
25 is too dark there, it seems. They would die, he said, before the roots were strong enough. Do you think he is right?"

"Maybe. He ought to know. He has been a gardener for more than twenty years. You'd better follow
30 his advice. If you don't you may regret it."

"Let's go in. It's getting chilly, and you have no jacket. If you caught cold you would never forgive me."

LXXX

(*a*) One winter-time, when I was sixteen, and Gregory nineteen, I was sent by my father on an errand to a place about seven miles distant by the road, but only about four by the mountains. He bade me return by the road, for the evenings closed in early, and were often thick and misty; besides, old Adam, now paralytic and bed-ridden, foretold a fall of snow before long. I soon got to my journey's end, and soon had done my business; earlier by an hour, I thought, than my father had believed, so I took the decision of the way by which I would return into my own hands, and set off back again over the mountains, just as the first shades of evening began to fall. It looked dark and gloomy enough; but everything was so still that I thought I should have plenty of time to get home before the snow came down. Off I set at a pretty quick pace. But night came on quicker. The path was clear enough in the day-time, although at several points two or three exactly similar diverged from the same place.

(*b*) Mrs. B. had gone to meet her daughter who was coming home for the holidays. Although the sky was grey she had not taken her mackintosh. She had only left herself twenty minutes or so to get to the station, which was over a mile away, and there was no means of getting there except by bus. She might have taken the car had it not been out of action.

When she reached the station her daughter had already been waiting for her for a few minutes, and was somewhat agitated. One does not expect one's mother to be late on such occasions. "I am very sorry," she said, "to have kept you waiting. I ought to have taken a taxi."

NOTES ON THE "O" AND "A" LEVEL PAPERS
LEVEL PAPERS

ITALIAN EDITION

SECTION III

NOTES

ORDINARY LEVEL

ABBREVIATIONS
NOTES ON PARTS OF THE VERB

As Italian Grammars written in English use a different nomen-
clature for parts of the verb, a short explanation is given below
of their names according to Italian usage.

Ger. Gerund (Italian *gerundio*). Ends in *-ando* for the first
conjugation, *-endo* for the second and third conjugations.
Translates the English form in "-ing", when referring to the
subject of the main clause: e.g. (II, 7) Maurice, holding the
duck, came out, *Maurizio, tenendo l'anitra, uscì.*

Pres.Part. Present Participle (Italian *participio presente*). Ends
in *-ante* sg., *-anti* pl. for the first conjugation; *-ente* sg.,
-enti pl. for the second and third conjugations. Translates the
English form in "-ing", when it has the force of an adjective:
e.g. (III, 4) winning numbers, *numeri vincenti.* See also
XLIV, 16.

P.Part. Past Participle (Italian *participio passato*).

Imp. Imperfect tense (Italian *imperfetto*). Also referred to as
"Past Descriptive". Describes habitual or progressive action
in the past, or the circumstances already existing when an
event occurred. Also in relative clauses which describe in the
past.

P.Def. Past Definite tense (Italian *passato remoto*). Also referred to as "Past Absolute" or "Past Historic". Places an
event in a certain moment of the past, isolating it from anything happening before or after. Used in formal narrative and
written prose, seldom in conversation.

NOTE. A detailed guide to the correct usage of the Imperfect
and the Past Definite is given in the notes to the first five
passages, and occasional notes are given in subsequent passages to show the correct usage of the two tenses: this is

extremely important and should be mastered from the early stages of the student's written work.

Perf. Perfect tense (Italian *passato prossimo*). This is the past tense most used in conversation, as it describes events happening recently and in some way connected with the present moment.

Plup. Pluperfect (Italian *trapassato prossimo*). Sometimes called "Past Perfect". Formed with the Imperfect of the auxiliary verb *avere* or *essere* and the Past Participle. Used in main clauses: e.g. they had spoken, *avevano parlato*, and in subordinate clauses introduced by conjunctions of time (*dopo che, quando, appena che*, etc.) with Imperfect or Perfect in the main clause: e.g. he relaxed when he (had) finished studying, *si riposava, quando aveva finito di studiare* or *si è riposato, quando aveva finito di studiare*.

P.Ant. Past Anterior (Italian *trapassato remoto*). Sometimes called "Second Past Perfect". Formed with the Past Definite of the auxiliary verb and the Past Participle. Not very often used, and then only in subordinate clauses introduced by conjunctions of time and describing a single action in the past, with Past Definite in the main clause: e.g. he relaxed when he (had) finished studying, *si riposò, quando ebbe finito di studiare*.

I

1 *To spend*, passare (of time. P. Def. See Abbreviations).
2 *On a farm*, in una fattoria. ("On" is often translated by *in* in the sense of "within": e.g. on the train, *nel treno*; and by *su* when indicating contact with a surface: e.g. on the chair, *sulla sedia*; on the beach, *sulla spiaggia*. The English word "factory" is *fabbrica* or *stabilimento*.)
3 *Everything that*, tutto quello che *or* tutto ciò che. (Always insert the pronoun *quello* or *ciò* between *tutto* and *che*.)
3 *On weekdays*, i giorni di lavoro *or* nei giorni di lavoro. (Before the days of the week "on" is expressed in Italian by the definite article: e.g. on Sunday, *la domenica*.)
4 *In the open air*, all'aria aperta. ("In" is translated by *a* in many expressions of place, time, manner, etc.: e.g. in

the light, *alla luce*; in the dark, *allo scuro* or *al buio*; in the morning, *al mattino*; in the evening, *alla sera*; in a fashionable way, *alla moda*; in pencil, *a matita*; in oils, *a olio*, etc.)

4, 5 *Got up, spent, played, helped.* (Imp. for habitual action, in this case normally happening on weekdays. See Abbreviations.)

6 *All the people*, tutti.

6, 7 *Were, was.* (Imp. for description.)

7 *In winter*, d'inverno. (*Di* is idiomatically used before names of seasons considered generally and not qualified: e.g. *d'estate*, in summer *or* in the summer; *d'autunno, di primavera*. *In autunno* and *in primavera* are also used. But: in the summer of 1957, *nell'estate del 1957*.)

7 *Covered with*, coperto di. ("With" is often translated by *di* after certain verbs and adjectives: e.g. to laugh with joy, *ridere di gioia*; to weep with shame, *piangere di vergogna*; armed with, *armato di*; filled with, *pieno di*; in love with, *innamorato di*, etc.)

8 *Did not work.* (Imp. for habitual action.)

9, 10 *Drove, bought.* (P.Def. The actions referred to are isolated in a definite moment of the past, i.e. "one morning".)

9 *To drive*, andare in automobile *or* andare in carrozza.

10 *It was.* (Imp.)

11 *There.* (Can be omitted.)

11 *On the way home*, sulla via di casa *or* tornando a casa.

11, 12 *Passed, stopped.* (P.Def.)

12 *To look at*, guardare. (No preposition required in Italian.)

12 *An old church*, una chiesa antica. ("Old" is *vecchio*, losing value because of age, and *antico*, gaining value because of age.)

13, 14 *Was pleased, was late, was tired.* (Imp.)

13 *When they got home*, di arrivare a casa. (English phrase "to get home".)

14, 15 *Went to bed, was . . . asleep.* (P.Def.)

15 *To be fast asleep*, addormentarsi profondamente.

15 *Soon*, subito. ("Soon" can be translated by *subito, fra poco, presto. Subito* means a short time after the previous

action or thought: e.g. the waiter soon came, *il cameriere venne subito* (after my call or intention of calling him); it means "immediately" or "at once". *Fra poco* refers to the future: e.g. the train is leaving soon, *il treno parte fra poco*. *Presto* means "within a short time, quickly"; e.g. I soon finished my work, *finii presto il mio lavoro*. *Presto* might also refer to future time.)

II

2 *To go on*, continuare *or* proseguire.

2 *Will you accept?* (Present of *accettare*, or Present of *volere* followed by Infinitive.)

3 *A few moments*, qualche momento. (*Qualche* is indeclinable and singular: e.g. a few birds were singing, *qualche uccello cantava*; a few people came, *qualche persona è venuta*.)

4 *Put it in his pocket*, se lo mise in tasca. (Reflexive pronoun *si* becomes *se* before *lo*, standing for *denaro*.)

NOTE. No possessive adjective is required before nouns indicating parts of the body or articles of clothing closely related to their owner: e.g. I put on my hat, *mi metto il cappello*; she washes her hands, *ella si lava le mani*. The reflexive pronoun indicates that the action is done to oneself.)

5 *Let us go back*. (First person plural Imperative of *ritornare*.)

6 *To come out of*, uscire da.

7 *Holding*, tenendo. (Ger. See Abbreviations.)

7 *His fingers burnt*, con le dita bruciate. (Many words indicating parts of the body are masculine in the sg. and feminine in the pl.: e.g. *il braccio*, *le braccia*, arms; *il dito*, *le dita*, fingers; *il labbro*, *le labbra*, lips, etc.)

8 *After putting back*, dopo aver rimesso. (Past Infinitive, the equivalent of "after having put back".)

11 *They would set out . . . and would follow*, sarebbero partiti e avrebbero seguito. (The Past Conditional here follows "decided that" understood.)

NOTE. Use of the tenses of the Conditional in a subordinate clause:

Modern Italian differs from English (and French) in one particular case in the use of the tenses of the Conditional. In a subordinate clause containing the Conditional after a verb of saying, believing, deciding, or an expression such as to be sure, certain, USED IN THE PAST TENSE, English language employs either *the simple Conditional*, when the statement has come true: e.g. he said he would come (and he did); or *the Past Conditional*, when the statement has not come true: e.g. he said he would have come (and he did not). Such a distinction does not exist in Italian. *Whether or not the statement has come true, after a verb in the past tense modern Italian always uses the Past Conditional.*

E.g. He SAID he would come ⎫
      or   ⎬ *Disse che sarebbe venuto.*
He SAID he would have ⎭
come

But, if the verb of saying, etc. is IN THE PRESENT TENSE, English and Italian have the same usage: e.g.

(1) He SAYS he would come (if he could), *dice che verrebbe* (Simple Conditional with an if-clause either expressed or understood, implying that the action is unlikely to happen);

(2) He says he would have come, *dice che sarebbe venuto* (Past Conditional. The action is unfulfilled).

Remember then:

    Disse che sarebbe venuto (for both simple and Past Conditional in English. Future in the Past)
    Dice che verrebbe (Pres. Cond. Improbable)
    Dice che sarebbe venuto (Past Cond. Action unfulfilled)

12 *To say good-bye to*, salutare *or* dire addio a. (Salutare, without preposition, is used on *meeting* or *leaving* some-somebody: *dire addio a* is only used on *leaving* somebody, generally for ever.)

15 *Was.* (Imp. All other past tenses in the passage are to be translated with P.Def.)

79

III

1 *To enter*, entrare in. (P.Def.)

1, 3 *Was working, held*. (Imp.)

2 *To talk about*, parlare di. (Imp.)

3 *In his hand*, in mano.

4 *Winning numbers*, numeri vincenti. (Pres. Part. See Abbreviations.)

4 *I've won nothing*, non ho vinto niente. (Perf.)

NOTE. A negative sentence beginning with *non* requires **two** negatives in Italian: e.g. I don't do anything, *non faccio niente*. (*Non* and *niente* are both negatives.)

5 *You*, tu (as the conversation takes place between two intimate friends).

5 *Any tickets*, dei biglietti. (Partitive construction. See X, 6.)

6 *I bought one*, ne ho comprato uno. (Perf. for past action in conversation. *Ne*, "of them", is understood in English, but must be expressed in Italian.)

6 *I don't remember*, non mi ricordo. (The verb *ricordare* and its opposite *dimenticare* can be used as reflexive verbs *ricordarsi* and *dimenticarsi* when one wants to emphasize the intimate connection between the subject and the action. In such cases they are followed by *di*: e.g. *egli si è ricordato di me, io mi dimentico di telefonare*.)

7 *I think I've lost it*, credo di averlo perduto.

NOTE. *Credo, penso, spero, desidero, decido, suppongo, temo*, etc. are followed by *di* and the Infinitive when both verbs refer to the same subject: e.g. I hope I will see her, *spero di vederla*. If the subject of the subordinate clause is different, such verbs are followed by *che* and the Subjunctive: e.g. I hope he is doing it, *spero che egli lo faccia*.

8 *Spoke* (Imp.); *took out, opened, noticed* (P.Def.).

10 *Pockets*, scompartimenti (of a wallet).

12, 13, 15 *Continued, heard, asked, exclaimed*. (P.Def.)

14 *Dreadfully pale*, mortalmente pallido.

15 *Him*, gli. (Dative or *indirect* object pronoun with the verb *domandare*.)

16 *The big prize*, il primo premio.

1 *To ask questions*, fare domande. (*Asked*, P.Def.)

1, 3 *He thought, did not like, knew.* (Imp.)

2 *In the world*, del mondo. ("In" is translated by *di* after a superlative: e.g. this is the oldest church in the town, *questa è la più antica chiesa della città.*)

3 *To like*, piacere. (The subject of "to like" becomes the indirect object—dative case—of *piacere*, while the object of the English verb becomes the subject of *piacere*, but nearly always follows the verb in Italian: e.g. Mary likes flowers, *a Maria piacciono i fiori*; he likes sport, *gli piace lo sport*; I should like to go out tonight, *mi piacerebbe uscire stasera.*)

4, 9 *Answered.* (P.Def.)

4 *Him*, gli. (*Indirect* object pronoun with the verb *rispondere.*)

7 *Was astonished, repeated.* (P.Def.)

8, 10 *Did you judge, saw.* (Perf.)

10 *Flourishing*, fiorente. (Pres. Part. See III, 4.)

11 *All of them*, tutti loro *or* loro tutti. (In this particular case *loro* can be omitted. "Of" between "all" and a *pronoun* is not translated: e.g. all of us, *tutti noi* or *noi tutti*; all of you, *tutti voi* or *voi tutti.*)

12 *Having*, avendo. (Ger.)

12 *Went out*, andò. (P.Def.)

13 *Helped.* (P.Def.)

13 *To drive out*, respingere.

15 *Was aroused*, fu suscitata. (P. Def.)

16 *Began.* (P.Def.)

16 *To think of*, pensare a.

17 *Could ask him*, avrebbe potuto fargli. (Past Conditional. See Note to II, 11.)

V

1 *Soon after three o'clock*, subito dopo le tre *or* poco dopo le tre. (After a number indicating the hours, *ore* is understood: e.g. it is nine o'clock, *sono le nove*.)

1 *It was still early*, era ancora presto.

2 *Decided to leave*, decise di lasciare. (See Note to III, 7.)

3 *His aunt*, sua zia. (The possessive adjective is used without article before names of relationship in the sg., not modified by a suffix, and not accompanied by an adjective: e.g. *mio fratello, sua figlia, nostro zio*; but *il mio fratellino, la sua cara figlia, i nostri zii. Loro*, "their" and "theirs", takes the article in any case: e.g. *la loro sorella, i loro cugini, le loro nipotine*.)

3, 4 *Worked, had.* (Imp.)

4 *More than*, più di. ("Than" after a comparative is translated by *di* before a noun, a pronoun and a number—as in this case—and by *che* before all other parts of speech.)

5 *First he stood*, dapprima si fermò.

6 *To hurry across the street*, attraversare in fretta la strada.

7 *To walk to the church*, camminare fino alla chiesa. (*Fino*, "as far as", is necessary between *camminare* and the noun indicating the *place* towards which one is walking.)

8 *Stood*, si elevava.

9 *Larger than*, più larghi che. ("Than" is *che* before the preposition *a*. See line 4 above.)

9 *At home*, normally *a casa*; but in this case *al suo paese* or *nella sua città* (in his own country or town).

10 *Looked at*, guardò. (P.Def.)

10 *In the windows*, nelle vetrine.

11 *Behind him*, dietro a lui.

VI

1 *To ring*, suonare alla porta *or* suonare il campanello. (*Alla porta* or *il campanello* are added for the sake of precision, because *suonare* in Italian is used for any instrument which

makes a sound: e.g. *suonare il piano, le campane, il claxon,* etc.)

1 *Came,* venne ad aprire. (*Venire* by itself would be too vague.)

1 *Him,* gli. (*Indirect* object pronoun with the verb *dire.*)

2 *To leave behind,* lasciare *or* dimenticare (in the sense of "to forget to take". *Lasciare dietro* means either literally to leave behind one something like smoke, perfume, or, figuratively, love, hatred, etc.: e.g. the train passed, leaving behind a puff of smoke, *il treno passò lasciandosi dietro un'ondata di fumo*; he went away, leaving behind him much regret, *partì lasciandosi dietro molto rimpianto.*)

2 *Guest,* ospite. (The same word also translates "host".)

5 *What is in the box?* Che c'è nella scatola? (*C'è*, which translates "is there" and "there is", is preferred to the simple *è* when followed by expressions indicating place: e.g. who is at home? *chi c'è a casa?*; many people are in the square, *c'è molta gente nella piazza.*)

6 *You should have opened it,* avresti dovuto aprirla. (The English simple Conditional is translated by the Past Conditional of *dovere* followed by the Present Infinitive in Italian. Similarly with *potere*: e.g. I could have done it, *avrei potuto farlo.*)

8 *The whole evening,* tutta la sera. (The whole afternoon, *tutto il pomeriggio,* etc.)

8 *Could not stop thinking about,* non poteva fare a meno di pensare a. (The idiomatic phrase *non posso fare a meno di* also translates "I cannot help".)

9 *The play,* la rappresentazione *or* lo spettacolo.

10 *To walk back,* ritornare a piedi.

10 *Having arrived,* arrivato (P.Part.) *or* dopo essere arrivato.

11 *To have a look at,* guardare *or* dare uno sguardo a.

12 *Light,* leggero (of weight), chiaro (of colour).

13 *While looking at it,* mentre la guardava *or* guardandola (Ger.)

13 *Suddenly,* improvvisamente. (Not *subito.* See I, 15.)

14 *His.* (Use the definite article, not the possessive adjective.)

15 *What,* quello che *or* ciò che. (The relative pronoun "what"

must always be translated in Italian by *two* pronouns, a demonstrative pronoun *quello* or *ciò* and the relative pronoun *che*.)

15 *To fill with*, riempire di. (See *pieno di*, I, 7.)

VII

1 *Stood*, stava *or* era. (Imp.)

2 *Near*, vicino a.

4 *To say to oneself*, dire fra sè. (I say to myself, you, etc., *dico fra me; tu . . . fra te; egli, ella, essi . . . fra sè. Fra noi, fra voi, fra loro* have a reciprocal meaning, "to each other".

4 *To go into*, entrare in. (See III, 1.)

5 *Of which*, di cui. (After a preposition the relative pronoun is always *cui* for persons or things: e.g. *con cui, a cui, da cui, per cui*, etc.)

7 *Footsteps*, rumore di passi.

8 *Putting down*, posato *or* dopo aver posato. (Past Infinitive because the meaning is "after having put down".)

9 *Were approaching*, si stavano avvicinando a.

NOTE. The construction of the verb *stare* followed by the Italian Gerund is the equivalent of the English progressive form of the verb, but its use is more limited than in English. Such a construction can only be used in Italian to emphasize the fact that the action was in progress at the time of speaking.

10 *There were five of them*, erano cinque.

13 *To succeed in*, riuscire a (conjugated with *essere*).

14 *The guides*, le guide. (The word *la guida* is always feminine and can be used to refer to a man or to a woman.)

14 *Soon*, fra poco *or* presto (referring to the future. See I, 15).

15 *To need somebody*, aver bisogno di qualcuno.

16, 17 *Would set out, would look for*, si sarebbero messi in cammino, avrebbero cercato. (Past Conditional. See Note to II, 11.)

VIII

1 *To sit down to table*, sedersi a tavola.

1, 2 *Had sat down, had not said*, si erano seduti, non aveva detto. (Plup. See Abbreviations.)

2 *About*, verso *or* circa a.

3 *To push back*, respingere.

5 *To be hungry*, avere fame. (Sensations of cold, hunger, etc., and feelings of fear, shame, etc., expressed in English with the verb "to be", are rendered in Italian with *avere*: e.g. to be cold, *avere freddo*; to be hot, *avere caldo*; to be thirsty, *avere sete*; to be sleepy, *avere sonno*; to be afraid, *avere paura*; to be ashamed, *avere vergogna*; to be patient, *avere pazienza*. The corresponding expressions with *essere* describe a permanent quality: e.g. *essere freddoloso, caloroso, pauroso* is to be in the habit of feeling cold, heat, fear; *essere vergognoso, paziente* is to be normally shy, patient.)

6 *To the great surprise*, con gran sorpresa. ("To" is translated by *con* in similar expressions: e.g. to their amazement, *con loro meraviglia*; to our joy, *con nostra grande gioia*. *Grande* may be added for euphony and emphasis.)

7 *To hear of*, sentir parlare di. (To hear from, *ricevere notizie da*.)

7 *Ever*, mai (meaning "sometimes"; "never" is *non . . . mai* or *giammai* in a negative sense.)

11 *To go and fetch*, andare a prendere.

12 *To go out of*, uscire da.

14 *The island you are speaking about*, l'isola di cui tu parli. (This literally means "about which you are speaking", as in Italian a sentence cannot end with a preposition.)

NOTE. The relative pronouns "which, that, what, who, whom", often understood in English, must always be expressed in Italian by *che*, subject and object pronoun, and by *cui* after a preposition: e.g. the man who speaks, *l'uomo che parla*; the man I saw, *l'uomo che ho visto*; the things you did, *le cose che hai fatto*; the town you come from, *la città da cui vieni*; the firm he works for, *la ditta per cui lavora*.

15 *Putting*, mettendo. (Ger., referring to the subject of the main clause.)

18 *He has bought.* (Equals "that he . . . ". "That", understood in English, must be expressed by *che*.)

18 *To have a house built*, farsi costruire una casa. ("To have something done" is translated by *fare* and the Infinitive, i.e. the *causative* use of *fare*: e.g. I am having some work done, *faccio fare un lavoro*; he had the thief punished, *fece punire il ladro*.)

IX

1 *Did not believe her*, non le credeva. (Imp.)

2, 4 *Had said, had wanted.* (Plup.)

3 *To drive . . . herself*, guidare lei stessa . . .

5 *To refuse to*, rifiutarsi di. (Plup.)

5 *No girl*, nessuna ragazza. (The negative pronoun *nessuno*, "nobody", is also a negative adjective, *nessuno, nessuna*. A negative clause beginning with *nessuno* does not require a second negative: e.g. nobody comes, *nessuno viene*.)

6 *Was old enough to drive till she was fifteen*, era in età di guidare fino a quindici anni *or* poteva guidare *or* riceveva il permesso di guidare fino all'età di quindici anni. (A more literal translation would be very clumsy.)

9 *Hoped.* (Imp.)

10 *Would not come back*, che non tornasse. (Subjunctive. See III, 7. Imperfect Subjunctive for sequence of tenses: e.g. *spero che egli venga*, where the Present tense is used in main and subordinate clause; *speravo che egli venisse*, using the Imperfect tense in both clauses.) The P. Conditional is also acceptable, *che non sarebbe tornato*.

11 *To shout good-bye to*, gridare addio a.

12 *To drive off*, partire.

13 *She would be able*, che avrebbe potuto. (P.Conditional. See Note to II, 11.)

15 *What a pity*, che peccato. (The indefinite article "a" after

the exclamatory "what" is not translated in Italian: e.g. what a fool! *che sciocco!*; what a question! *che domanda!*)

16 *Was not watching her*, non la guardasse. (Imp. Subjunctive after "what a pity that", *che peccato che*.)

X

1 *To have to*, dovere. ("To have" and "to be" followed by "to" and the Infinitive are translated by *dovere*: e.g. we have to go, *dobbiamo andare*; I am to wait here, *devo aspettare qui*.)

1 *To get up*, alzarsi.

1 *On the following morning*, l'indomani mattina. (*Domani mattina* means "tomorrow morning". See line 4.)

2 *To leave*, partire da (in the sense of "to set out from").

3 *Before going*, prima di andare. (All prepositions in Italian are followed by the Infinitive of a verb.)

6 *Some students*, alcuni studenti *or* degli studenti *or* studenti. (The partitive "some" and "any" are translated by the adjective *alcuno*, or by *di* and the definite article, or can be omitted.)

7 *To play a joke*, fare uno scherzo.

9 *It appeared that*, sembrava che (and Imp. Subjunctive).

9 *Both men*, tutti e due gli uomini. (Between *tutti* and a cardinal number *e* must be inserted: e.g. all four, *tutti e quattro*.)

11 *Then*, allora. ("Then" is translated by *allora* when it means "at that moment" or when it implies an idea of cause and effect, over and above the idea of time: e.g. *noi siamo pronti, allora cominciamo*.)

11 *To knock . . . on the door*, bussare alla porta.

12 *Was on fire*, stava bruciando.

12 *To go on*, continuare a.

14 *To jump out of bed*, saltare dal letto.

14 *To look at one's face in the mirror*, guardarsi allo specchio.

1 *The poor man*, il pover'uomo. (If *povero* is placed after *uomo*, it means a "needy man".)

1 *At that time*, a quel tempo. ("Time" may also be translated by *volta* and *ora*. *Volta* = occasion: e.g. three times, *tre volte*; *ora* = time on the clock: e.g. it is time to go home, *è ora di andare a casa*.)

5 *To make one's way towards*, avviarsi verso *or* dirigersi verso.

6 *To be not very far away*, non essere molto lontano *or* lontana.

9 *To begin by*, cominciare da *or* cominciare con.

10 *Then*, poi. ("Then" is translated by *poi* in speaking of a series of actions.)

11 *To owe somebody a debt*, aver un debito verso qualcuno.

NOTE. In phrases with a compound tense and "for", indicating an action which started in the past and which has continued up to the moment of speaking, the Italian usage is a simple tense and *da*: e.g. I have waited for an hour, *aspetto da un'ora*; he had lived in England for ten years, *abitava in Inghilterra da dieci anni*.)

12 *Did not know*, non sapeva. (Imp.)

13 *Could, heard*. (Imp.)

13 *Scarcely*, sì e no *or* a stento *or* difficilmente.

13 *Believe what*, credere a quello che. (See VI, 15.)

14 *Never*, non . . . mai. (See VIII, 7.)

15 *I promised*, ho promesso. (Perf.)

15 *To remember your goodness*, di ricordarmi della tua bontà. (See III, 6.)

15 *To me*, verso di me.

16 *What*, qualsiasi *or* qualunque (the equivalent of "whatsoever").

1 *In London*, a Londra. (*A* before towns indicates residence in, or motion to: e.g. we live in Rome, *abitiamo a Roma*; I go to Milan, *vado a Milano*.)

1 *Late in the evening*, la sera tardi.

2 *Early next morning*, la mattina dopo, presto.

5 *After he had whistled . . . a face appeared*, dopo che ebbe fischiato . . . apparì una faccia. (P.Ant. in subordinate clause, with P.Def. in main clause. See Abbreviations.)

6 *To go for a walk*, andare a fare una passeggiata. ("To stroll", *andare a spasso* or *andare a passeggio*.)

7 *I'm looking for*, sto cercando. (See VII, 9.)

11 *They had no*, non avevano. (Imp. for reported speech in the past.)

13 *As fast as they could*, il più rapidamente possibile *or* il più presto possibile.

XIII

3 *Lying*, disteso. (Where the English form in "-ing" expresses a state, not an action, Italian uses the Past Participle: e.g. he is sitting, *è seduto*; kneeling, *inginocchiato*.)

4 *To waste no time*, non perdere tempo.

4 *Took off his coat*, si levò il soprabito. (See Note to II, 4.)

7 *To fetch*, andare *or* venire a prendere. (In this case use *venire*, which means "approach" between the speaker and the person to whom one speaks.)

8 *To fall ill*, ammalarsi.

9 *He had to go*, è dovuto andare. (Perf. See X, 1.)

10 *It rained.* (Imp.)

10 *To get wet*, bagnarsi. (Perf. "To bathe" is *fare un bagno*.)

11 *It was very cold*, faceva molto freddo. ("To be" is translated by *fare* used impersonally in some expressions describing the weather: e.g. it is hot, *fa molto caldo*; it is cool, *fa fresco*; it is fine, *fa bel tempo*, etc.)

12 *By then*, allora. (See X, 11.)

12 *Not to feel well*, non sentirsi bene *or* sentirsi male.

13 *He seemed worse*, sembrava peggiorato *or* stava peggio. ("Worse" and "better" can be translated by *peggio* and *meglio* as adverbs, by *peggiore* and *migliore* as adjectives: e.g. he is better, *sta meglio*; he is a better man, *è un uomo migliore*; it is worse, *è peggio*; he is a worse student, *è uno studente peggiore*. *Il meglio, il peggio* are used as nouns: e.g. for better, for worse, *per il meglio, per il peggio*.

    Peggiorato and *migliorato* are Past Parts. of the verbs *peggiorare* and *migliorare*, "to become worse" and "to ameliorate".)

13 *He was dying*, che stesse morendo *or* che morisse. (Imp. Subjunctive for correct sequence of tenses after "I thought".)

14 *Went to see you*, sono venuta a cercarla *or* la sono venuta a cercare.

15 *If only we were* . . . *!* se soltanto fossimo . . . ! (Imp. Subj. in an if-clause, where the condition is unfulfilled.)

XIV

1 *Dared not*, non osava. (Imp.)

1 *To stay away*, non andarci. (To play truant is *marinare la scuola*.)

4 *Without* . . . *or*, senza . . . nè (and Infinitive).

5 *How glad she was!* Come fu contenta! *or* Quanto fu contenta! (Note the different order of words in Italian. "How" in exclamatory expressions is translated by *che* before adjectives: e.g. how beautiful! *che bello!*, by *come* or *quanto* before a verb or an adverb: e.g. how tall she is! *come* or *quanto è alta!* how quickly! *come* or *quanto rapidamente!*)

6 *To be over*, finire.

7 *Avoiding*, evitando. (Ger.)

7 *To hurry into the street*, correre nella strada *or* in strada.

8 *Used to*, era solito *or* aveva l'abitudine di.

10 *To go away*, andarsene.

11 *To her aunt*, dalla zia. (*Andare* and *venire* are followed by *da*, meaning "at the house of", before names of relations, personal pronouns, and names of traders or professional people: e.g. I'll go to my cousin's, *andrò da mio cugino*; will you come to see me? *verrai da me?*; she went to the hairdresser's, *andò dal parrucchiere*; they have gone to the doctor's, *sono andati dal dottore*.)

11 *For a year she had saved*. (Imp. of *risparmiare* followed by *da*. See Note to XI, 11.)

13 *To wonder*, chiedersi *or* domandarsi.

13 *I know!* Ecco!

13 *To go and see*, andare a trovare *or* andare da.

XV

1 *Good-bye, mother*, ciao, mamma. (*Ciao* is the way of greeting very intimate friends, relations and children, when either meeting or leaving them.)

1 *To visit*, andare a far visita a *or* andare a trovare. (*Visitare* is used for a doctor visiting a patient, a personality making an official visit or anybody visiting an exhibition or a church.)

2 *He must be ill*, deve essere malato *or* sarà malato. (The Future may be used to express doubt or probability.)

2, 6 *Was not, was*. (Imp.)

3 *To hurry along*, affrettarsi lungo. (P.Def.)

5 *Let him in*, lo fece entrare. (P.Def.)

6 *To go up to*, salire a.

8 *Had seen*, avevano visto. (Plup.)

9 *Shortly afterwards*, poco dopo.

12 *Although Peter was*, sebbene Pietro fosse. (Subj. after *sebbene*.)

13 *To ask for something to eat*, chiedere *or* domandàre qualcosa da mangiare.

XVI

1 *Were.* (Imp.)
2 *At once,* subito. (See VI, 13.)
2 *Night had already fallen,* si era già fatto scuro (Impersonal use of *fare* for expressions of weather; see XIII, 11) *or* la notte era già scesa (more poetical).
4 *To go down,* scendere in.
5 *Empty,* libero.
5 *Towards him,* verso di lui. ("Towards" followed by a pronoun is *verso di*: e.g. towards me, *verso di me*; "towards" followed by a noun is *verso*: e.g. towards the town, *verso la città.*)
7 *To wait for,* aspettare (without preposition).
7 *To come and see me,* venire da me *or* venire a trovarmi.
12 *To read again,* rileggere *or* leggere di nuovo.
12 *Would he come?* sarebbe venuto? (P.Cond. See Note to II, 11.)
13 *Why Charles had chosen,* perchè Carlo avesse scelto. (The Subj. is preferable to the Indicative in indirect questions like this one.)
14 *As he was putting back . . . into his pocket,* mentre stava rimettendosi in tasca. . . . (See Note to VII, 9.)
15 *The door opened,* la porta s'aprì. (Reflexive verb.)

XVII

1 *Sharply,* bruscamente *or* di colpo.
2 *Shutters,* persiane.
3 *Still,* ancora. (*Ancora* also means "again".)
4 *Who is there?* Chi è là? (as a challenge) *or* chi c'è? ("who is at home?")
4 *What do you want?* cosa volete? (The *voi* gives a general idea of people.)
7 *To lock,* chiudere a chiave.
8 *Walk,* cammino (noun) *or* a camminare (verb).

8 *To retrace his steps*, ritornare sui suoi passi *or* ritornare indietro.

11, 12 *Would be able, would give him*, sarebbero stati capaci di, gli avrebbero dato.

12 *Information*, informazioni. (The Italian word *informazione* has in the singular a specified meaning of a piece of news, and in the plural a more general meaning.)

14 *It's no doubt*, senza dubbio è *or* non c'è dubbio che sia.

15 *She has been living there for*, abita lì da. (See Note to XI, 11.)

16 *At least*, per lo meno.

17 *As herself*, come lei.

XVIII

1 *Has happened?* è successo?

2 *Hearing*, udendo.

2 *To realize*, rendersi conto di *or* accorgersi di (in the sense of "understanding". "To realize" may be translated by *realizzare* or *effettuare* in the sense of "to make real").

3 *Who she was*, chi ella fosse. (Subj. in indirect question.)

3 *Clearly*, evidentemente.

3 *She did not remember him*, ella non si ricordava di lui.

5 *To stop*, fermarsi. (The auxiliary with reflexive verbs is *essere*.)

7 *Any danger*, nessun pericolo.

8 *To be late*, fare tardi *or* essere in ritardo. (*Fare tardi* indicates the "action" of being late, for which one is responsible; *essere in ritardo*, the "fact" of being late for which one might not be responsible. Use *fare tardi* here.)

9 *Could not help laughing*, non potè fare a meno di ridere. (See VI, 8.)

11 *To know*, conoscere (in the sense of "being acquainted with".)

13 *Would give . . . and amuse*, avrebbe dato . . . e si sarebbe divertito.

16 *Former companions*, i compagni di un tempo *or* di una volta.

17 *To think of*, pensare di (meaning "to have an opinion about"; *pensare a* is "to think of": e.g. I think of him, *penso a lui*.)

XIX

1 *To make an excursion into the country*, fare una scampagnata. ("Excursion" is normally *gita*, "trip"; the Italian word *escursione* is applied to climbing mountains or exploring a country.)

2 *Very early*, molto presto.

3 *To leave the house*, uscire di casa (in the sense of "getting out of" the house.)

9 *To get out*, scendere da (from a train, a bus, etc.)

10 *In the shade*, all'ombra. (See I, 4.)

11 *To have lunch*, fare colazione *or* mangiare.

11, 12 *Broke through, shone*. (Imp. To break through, *attraversare*.)

13 *They bathed*, fecero il bagno. (P.Def. See XIII, 10.)

XX

1 *To make somebody worry*, preoccupare qualcuno *or* rendere preoccupato qualcuno.

2 *Received*. (Imp.)

4 *There must be*, ci doveva essere. (Imp.)

4 *Something strange*, qualcosa di strano.

4 *About this one*, riguardo a questa (*lettera* understood).

5 *He went on turning it over and over in his hand*, continuava a girarla e rigirarla in mano.

8 *To put down on*, appoggiare su *or* posare su.

8 *He took off . . . and put them on top of it*, si levò . . . e glieli mise sopra.

9 *To pick up again*, riprendere.

11 *To strike the table with the hand*, dare un pugno sul tavolo.

11 *When my mother had finished*, quando mia madre la finì.
(The English Plup. is rendered here by the P.Def., as the
two actions of "finishing the letter" and "her face being
red" do not happen in a sequence of time, one after the
other, but at the same moment "at the end of the letter".

13 *Why (they) were*, perchè fossero. (Subj. in indirect
question.)

14 *When I had read it*, quando la ebbi letta *or* quando la lessi.
(The P.Ant. *la ebbi letta* indicates that the reading preceded the understanding; the P.Def. *la lessi* that the reading and the understanding were simultaneous. The second
interpretation is more vivid.)

XXI

1 *What to do*, che cosa fare.

1 *Can . . . be?* può essere? *or* sarà? (See XV, 2.)

2 *It is strange that*, è strano che (and Present Subj.)

6 *Along the pavement*, lungo il marciapiede.

8 *To ring*, telefonare *or* chiamare al telefono.

9 *To let her know*, per farle sapere.

9 *He would be late*, avrebbe fatto tardi.

12 *Was able to find*, potè trovare. (P.Def.)

13 *Behind him*, dietro a sè. (*sè*, "himself", not *lui* which
would mean somebody else.)

14 *Are you doing?* fai? *or* stai facendo? (See Note to VII, 9.)

XXII

3 *Did not want*, non voleva. (Imp.)

8 *Without getting tired*, senza stancarmi.

10 *On the other side*, dall'altra parte.

13 *To creep downstairs*, scendere le scale furtivamente *or* piano
piano.

13 *As*, mentre (= "while").
14 *Was striking two*, suonava le due.

XXIII

1 *As*, poichè (= "since").
3 *Homework*, compiti. ("Housework", *faccende domestiche.*)
4 *Detective story*, romanzo giallo.
4 *Which he took*, che aveva preso *or simply* preso. (Plup. or
P.Part. as the action of taking the book is previous to the
one of opening it.)
5 *Into the kitchen*, in cucina (idiomatically used without
definite article, like *in casa, in giardino, in terrazza, in
cantina*, "in the cellar".)
7 *He was sitting . . . when*, stava seduto *or* era seduto . . .
quando. (See XIII, 3.)
8 *To hear*, sentire (a noise of any kind. *Udire* is rather
poetical.)
10 *To put down*, posare.
10 *To hurry to*, correre a.
10 *Front door*, porta di fronte *or* porta principale (literally.
But *porta* by itself is a better rendering, as in Italy houses
seldom have front and back doors and so the language has
no equivalent expression.)
11 *In the light of the moon*, al lume di luna.
12 *Lying*, che giaceva. (See XLIV, 16 and LV, 3.)

XXIV

2 *Could not go to sleep*, non poterono addormentarsi.
3 *(They) lay awake*, rimasero svegli.
4 *A score*, una ventina.
4 *Took their guns*, si armarono. ("Guns" could be translated by *rivoltelle*, "revolvers", *fucili*, "rifles", or *armi da
fuoco* in a general sense.)
6 *Firing*, facendo fuoco su *or* sparando a.

6 *Moved*, si muoveva. (Reflexive verb.)

10 *Anything*, qualche cosa.

10 *By day*, di giorno *or* durante il giorno.

13 *To meet*, incontrarsi (reflexive form with reciprocal meaning, "each other".)

14 *Trembling with*, tremanti di (Pres.Part. with the force of an adjective) *or* tremando (Ger.).

16 *To grow silent*, divenire silenzioso.

XXV

1 *Every few hundred yards*, ogni cento metri.

1 *I came to*, io arrivavo a.

5 *In the sunshine*, al sole.

5 *There was no one to be seen*, non si vedeva nessuno.

8 *That someone was looking out at me*, che qualcuno mi guardasse.

10 *To*, in. (The order of words in Italian: "to what sort . . .").

11 *To make up one's mind*, decidere di.

12 *To be lost*, essersi perduto *or* aver perso la strada. (*Essere perduto* is used in a moral sense.)

13 (*I*) *should have*, avrei dovuto.

XXVI

3 *Them to me*, me le. (The indirect object pronoun *mi* becomes *me* before another pronoun.)

8 *It was thought that he knew*, si pensava che egli conoscesse.

9 *Would pay*, avrebbe pagato.

14 *On foot*, a piedi.

16 *A ticket to Toronto*, un biglietto per Toronto. (*Per*, after certain nouns and verbs, indicates direction or destination: e.g. the road to Naples, *la strada per Napoli*; the train to Genoa, *il treno per Genova*; to leave for the country, *partire per la campagna*. It can also translate "through": e.g. to walk through the square, *camminare per la piazza*.)

XXVII

5 *Seemed to be*, sembrava essere *or* sembrava. ("To be" can be omitted.)

7 *To escape*, uscire da (speaking of smoke. Compare English "to issue".)

8 *Soon*, ben presto. (See I, 15. *Ben*, short for *bene*, gives some emphasis to *presto* and makes it sound better at the beginning of a sentence.)

13 *Would go away*, sarebbero andati via.

14 *We had no longer*, non avevamo più.

14 *Any*. (Not to be translated.)

15 *Would not be able*, non avrebbero potuto.

XXVIII

1 *Told*, lo disse a. (The verb *dire* must have an expressed direct object, in this case *lo*.)

1 *To call to somebody*, chiamare qualcuno.

4 *I went out in front of the class, and counted*, uscii dal banco (*banco* must be expressed to avoid vagueness) e contai davanti alla classe. (It is better to make "in front of the class" a complement of "counted".)

7 *Stop*, basta.

8 *Not to succeed in*, non riuscire a.

12 *To make somebody angry*, fare arrabbiare qualcuno *or* rendere qualcuno infuriato.

12 *Home*, a casa. (*A casa* indicates either motion to or rest at one's home.)

13 *I left the school*, uscii di scuola *or* da scuola. ("To leave" the house, the office, the shop, etc. is *uscire di casa* or *da casa, dall'ufficio, dal negozio*, etc. See X, 2 and XIX, 3.)

14 *To set out on one's way*, dirigersi verso.

14 *I was afraid . . . would be*, temevo che . . . si sarebbero arrabbiati.

2 *To board the train*, salire sul treno. (Compare *scendere da*, XIX, 9.)

3 *To be about to leave*, stare per partire.

5 *Platform*, marciapiede (in a railway station).

6 *Fellow-traveller*, compagno di viaggio.

6 *To call to*, chiamare (without preposition).

6 *I say!* Scusi!

7 *To miss*, perdere (meaning "not to catch". But "to miss" meaning "to feel the absence or loss" of something or someone is *sentire la mancanza di*.)

10 *To draw out*, mettersi in moto (of a train).

10 *He dropped (himself)*, si lasciò cadere.

11, 12 *Seat . . . seat*, posto . . . sedile. (*Posto*, a place for which one buys a ticket: e.g. *posti al teatro, in autobus, in treno*, etc. *Sedile*, something to sit on: e.g. there are seats in the garden, *ci sono sedili nel giardino*.)

11 *A thought occurred to me*, mi venne un pensiero *or* mi venne un'idea.

13 *It doesn't matter . . . that*, non importa . . . che (and Subj.).

XXX

2 *And that was all*, e basta.

5 *To lead a life*, condurre una vita *or* fare una vita. (*Fare una vita* is more familiar.)

5 *Why shouldn't I?* Perchè non avrei dovuto? *or* Perchè non dovevo?

7 *Terminal marks*, voti finali.

8 *To work*, studiare. (*Lavorare* cannot be used, as it refers to work done with the hands or in order to earn money.)

9 *To become angry*, arrabbiarsi.

13 *I should have liked*, mi sarebbe piaciuto.

14 *By.* (Not to be translated.)

15 *I should have to go back*, avrei dovuto ritornare (Conditional for probability) *or* dovevo ritornare (Indicative for reality).

16 *What is the matter?* Cosa c'è? *or* Cos'hai? (tu) *or* Cos'ha? (lei).

17 *To look sad,* sembrare triste.

XXXI

1 *To dress,* vestirsi (reflexive verb).

5 *In the mountains,* in montagna.

8 *Quite cool,* molto fresca (l'aria).

9 *Before we had breakfast.* (Do not translate "we had".)

12 *By the stream,* lungo il ruscello *or* vicino al ruscello.

13 *On the ground,* per terra. (Similarly "on the floor" is translated by *per terra.*)

14 *Soon,* poco dopo *or* dopo poco (as future in the past. As real future, "soon" is *fra poco* or *presto.* See I, 15.)

XXXII

1 *Knew,* conosceva. ("To know" is either *conoscere* or *sapere. Conoscere* means "to be acquainted with" or "to know" something more *complex* than a single thing or fact; e.g. do you know Mrs. Rossi? *conosce la signora Rossi?*; you know the town, *lei conosce la città. Sapere* means "to know a thing or a fact" or "to have learnt": e.g. I know she is ill, *so che è malata.*)

2 *To be drowned,* annegare *or* morire annegato (with *essere*).

3 *To bring up a child,* allevare *or* tirare su un bambino. (*Tirare su* is rather colloquial, but very expressive. To be preferred here.)

4 *As best she could,* nel miglior modo possibile *or* come meglio poteva *or* potè. (Compare "as fast as they could", XII, 13.)

7 *Prepared,* si preparavano. (Reflexive.)

7 *To go down to,* scendere a.

10 *Voyage,* viaggio di mare *or* viaggio. (The same word

viaggio translates the English words "travel, journey, voyage".)

12 *To enjoy something*, godere di una cosa.
12 *Open-air life*, vita all'aria aperta.
13 *To earn one's living*, guadagnarsi la vita.
15 *To laugh at*, ridere di.
16 *To keep on saying*, continuare a ripetere *or* ripetere continuamente.

XXXIII

1 *This is how*, ecco come.
3 *He set out*, si era incamminato. (Plup., the equivalent of "he had set out".)
5 *How to find his way back*, come ritornare.
11 *He heard them say*, sentì che essi dicevano.
13 *Asking to be given*, chiedendo che gli fosse dato (passive), *or* chiedendo che gli dessero (active).

XXXIV

9 *I won't let you go!* Non ti lascio andare *or* Non ti dò il permesso di andare.
13 *At the end of two hours*, dopo due ore.
18 *To crash*, precipitare (of planes or of any weight falling rapidly, generally ending in disaster).

XXXV

4 *Soon after*, subito dopo.
5 *To pull someone out of bed*, tirare qualcuno giù dal letto.
7 *Don't be an ass*, non fare lo stupido. (*Asino* is generally used for somebody not clever at school or in matters requiring brainwork.)

XXXVI

1 *On the evening before Christmas*, la sera della vigilia di Natale.

1 *A small boy*, un ragazzino.

2 *The snow lay deep*, la neve era alta *or* giaceva alta.

3 *On the ground*, sul terreno. (Here the description has a quality of precision well rendered by the literal translation *sul terreno*, and which could not be expressed by the more general, idiomatic phrase, *per terra.* See XXXI, 13.)

4 *Since the breakfast*, dal momento della colazione *or* dopo la colazione. ("Since" translated by *da* must be followed in Italian by a word indicating time, like *momento* or *quando*: e.g. since I met you, *da quando ti ho incontrato.*)

5 *Friendly*, cortese *or* gentile.

6 *Where he could sleep*, dove poter dormire.

7 *Quite alone*, proprio solo. (*Proprio* as adverb is very often used to give emphasis to the word immediately following. It can be translated in English by "quite, really, very", etc.)

7 *In the world*, al mondo.

8 (*They*) *died*, erano morti. (Plup., the equivalent of "had died".)

8 *Quite young*, molto giovane. ("Quite" = "very", *molto.*)

10 *In the distance*, in lontananza.

11 *Christmas carol*, canto di Natale.

13 *He was sitting*, si trovò seduto. ("Was" = "found himself").

XXXVII

2, 15 *Loudly, louder*, forte, più forte (of sounds).

3 *Help!* Aiuto!

4 *Increasingly*, sempre più.

4 *A mad woman*, una pazza. (The adjective in Italian can often have the force of a substantive.)

8 *It would not yield,* non cedeva. (The Imp. in Italian is
  sufficient to express the idea of resistance contained in
  "would not".)
10 *Was to have started,* doveva incominciare.
15 *I knew,* riconobbi. ("To know" is neither *conoscere* nor
   sapere in this case, but *riconoscere,* "to recognize".)

XXXVIII

1 *As a boy,* da ragazzo.
7 *Hither and thither,* di qua e di là.
15 *A thought struck him,* gli venne un pensiero *or* un pensiero
   lo colpì.

XXXIX

1 *Before long,* ben presto (in the sense of "very soon") *or*
  prima che passasse molto tempo. (A verb is necessary in
  a more literal translation.)
2 *I wished.* (Imp. Subj. after the indefinite antecedent
  "wherever".)
2 *The three of us,* noi tre.
4 *To send word,* fare avvertire *or* mandare a dire.
6 *As,* dato che *or* visto che.
7 *The matter,* la faccenda.
8 *On school holidays,* durante le vacanze di scuola. (One or
  a few days of holiday are called *giorni di festa.* The long
  holidays for office or shop workers are called *ferie.*)
13 *To enjoy oneself,* divertirsi.
14 *Could tell,* raccontava.
16 *One fine day,* un bel giorno.
17 *To come across someone,* venire addosso a uno.

5 *To make my horse enter the water*, fare entrare il mio cavallo nell'acqua.

6 *Unwillingly*, contro voglia *or* di mala voglia *or* malvolentieri.

6 *As soon as he had entered it*, appena entrato.

8 *To swim across it*, attraversarlo a nuoto.

12 *Six metres long*, lungo sei metri. ("Three metres wide", *largo tre metri*, etc.)

13 *To be about to bathe*, stare per buttarsi nell'acqua.

SECTION IV

NOTES

ADVANCED LEVEL

XLI

2 *By my own hearth,* vicino al mio caminetto. ("Own" is not to be translated.)

2, 3 *Smoking . . . and nodding,* fumando . . . e sonnecchiando. (Ger.)

4 *Upstairs,* di sopra.

4 *The locking of the hall door,* la porta d'ingresso che veniva serrata *or* chiusa a chiave (= "the hall door being locked". *Chiusura,* literal translation of "locking", is an abstract noun preferably used figuratively: e.g. *la chiusura delle scuole,* the closing-down of schools.)

5 *Some time before,* poco prima.

5 *Told me,* mi fece capire *or* mi avvertì. (*Dire,* "to tell", is to express by words.)

7 *To knock out the ashes of the pipe,* scuotere la cenere della pipa.

10 *At so late an hour,* ad un'ora così tarda.

11 *An all-night sitting,* una chiamata per tutta la notte.

11 *With a wry face,* con un viso contrariato *or* con una smorfia di scontento.

13 *Who stood upon my step,* alla mia porta *or* davanti alla mia porta.

15 *I hoped that I might not be too late,* speravo di non essere arrivato troppo tardi. ("To hope that", see III, 7.)

16 *To catch you,* per trovarti.

18 *Nothing but,* solamente.

19 *Brought*, fatto venire.

NOTE. The causative use of *fare* is very frequent in Italian and it lends itself to different shades of meaning, from the main idea of "having something done" (see VIII, 18), to that of "helping somebody" in doing something: e.g. *gli faccio fare la visita della città*, I take him round the city.

21 *As much jewellery as*, tanti gioielli quanti.

24 *However fast*, per quanto rapidamente (and Imp. Subj.).

25 *Fast enough to catch up with*, abbastanza rapidamente da raggiungere.

26 *Had succeeded in*, riuscì a. (P.Def. to be preferred. See XX, 14.)

27 *Weeping with*, piangendo di.

28 *The latter*, questi. ("The former . . . the latter", *quello . . . questi* or *il primo . . . il secondo*, in formal speech.)

XLII

1 *To mention the time*, accennare all'ora *or* dire l'ora. (*Menzionare* is rather stilted in Italian.)

1 *Before*, prima che (and Imp.Subj.).

2 *We should start*, saremmo partiti.

3 *To travel to*, viaggiare verso.

3 *I kept wishing that I had done so*, continuavo a desiderare di averlo fatto.

7 *Connection*, coincidenza (of trains).

8 *So much less . . . so far more*, molto meno . . . tanto più *or* tanto meno . . . quanto più. (The sentence becomes more effective by inserting a *ma* or *però* before the second "so".)

8 *Sensible*, pratico *or* di buon senso. (The Italian word *sensibile* means "sensitive".)

10, 11 *We were, were*. (P.Def.)

11 *To be in the way*, ingombrare *or* riuscire ingombrante.

12 *Until they were*, finchè furono. (Indicative. Equals "until the moment when . . .")

12 *To leave behind*. (See VI, 2.)

13 *To be gone*, essersi perso *or* essersi perduto.

16 *If . . . I should . . .*

NOTE. In Italian a Conditional sentence indicating probability or possibility requires *se* and Imp. or Plup. Subj. in the if-clause, and Pres. or P.Conditional in the main clause: e.g. if you worked hard, you would succeed, *se tu lavorassi molto, riusciresti*; if you had worked hard, you would have succeeded, *se tu avessi lavorato molto, saresti riuscito.*

18 *To be allowed,* avere il permesso di *or* è permesso di. (*È permesso* is preceded by indirect object: e.g. she is not allowed to play, *a lei non è permesso di giocare*; we are not allowed these things, *non ci sono permesse queste cose.* See Note to XLV,17 and similar construction of *piacere*, IV, 3.)

XLIII

1, 2 *There must be,* c'è sempre (in the sense of "there is always").

1 *Competition,* concorrenza.

4, 7 *May . . . may,* può (and Infinitive) . . . può darsi che (and Present Subj.).

6 *To believe that.* (See Note to III, 7.)

8 *To afford,* offrire *or* fornire (in the sense of "to supply". "To afford" referring to time is *disporre di* or *avere disponibile*: e.g. I cannot afford two hours, *non dispongo di due ore* or *non ho due ore disponibili.* "To afford" referring to money is *potersi permettere di* or *potersi permettere il lusso di* or *avere il denaro per*: e.g. he cannot afford a car, *non può permettersi (il lusso) di avere un'automobile*; we cannot afford to keep the boy at school, *non abbiamo il denaro per mantenere il ragazzo a scuola.*)

9 *All the time,* in continuazione *or* sempre.

9 *It is shown,* si vede.

10 (*It*) *is true of,* sì può dire di.

19 *To creep into,* infiltrarsi in.

21 *Believing himself to be,* credendosi *or* credendo di essere.

22 *Than he was*, di quanto non fosse. (*Di quanto* is necessary in Italian as second part of the comparison, *non* is pleonastic.)

22 *Was counting*, stava contando. (See Note to VII, 9.)

25 *Had had prepared for her*, si era fatta preparare. (See Note to XLI, 19.)

25, 26 *As soon as she had washed . . . had put*. (Plup.)

28 *Removed her nose*, le portò via il naso.

XLIV

3, 4 *Before . . . appeared . . . and asked*, prima che . . . (and Imp. Subj.).

6 *Went*, è andato. (Perf.)

7 *Never mind that*, non importa *or* non fa niente.

8 *News to give him*, notizie da dargli.

12 *To lead to something*, essere di grande importanza *or* essere di molta conseguenza.

14 *Of Polani himself*, dello stesso Polani *or* proprio la voce di Polani.

15 *Was heard*, si sentì. (In Italian the reflexive *si* is preferred to the passive voice: e.g. a lot of work was done, *si fece molto lavoro*, better than *molto lavoro fu fatto*.)

15 *At the top of*, in cima a.

16 *Stairs*, scalinata.

16 *Inquiring*, che domandava. (The Pres. Part. is here translated by a relative clause, as it has verbal function.)

19 *Would come*, sarebbe venuto. (Past Cond. See Note to II, 11.)

19 *Unless . . . were*, a meno che . . . non fossero. (*Non* is pleonastic.)

21 *It is I*, sono io. (*Sei tu, siamo noi, siete voi*, but *è lui, è lei, sono loro*.)

1 *To produce*, mettere in scena *or* rappresentare (a play).
2 *To seize the opportunity*, approfittare dell'occasione.
6 *Room*, posto *or* spazio.
7 *If something were not done, they would have to* se non si fosse fatto qualcosa, essi avrebbero dovuto. (See Note to XLII, 16.)
9 *The burning*, l'incendio.
11 *Regardless of*, senza riguardo a *or* senza riguardo verso.
12 *Flew*, volavano. (Imp.)
13 *Among . . . and . . . alike*, sia fra . . . che fra *or* tanto fra . . . che fra.
15 *No performance at all*, nessuna rappresentazione.
17 *The soldier was given*, al soldato fu dato *or* si diede.
NOTE. With the verbs "to be given, to be told, to be allowed", in the passive voice, the subject becomes the indirect object—dative case—in Italian. The verb is either in the passive voice or in the active preceded by the reflexive *si*, third person singular or plural: e.g. I am told a story, *mi si racconta una storia*; I am told many things, *mi si dicono molte cose*.
21 *He ought not to have come*, non avrebbe dovuto venire. ("Ought" has the same construction as "should, would, could". See VI, 6.)

XLVI

1 *To show into*, introdurre in *or* far passare in.
2 *Sat*. (Imp.)
4 *Whiskers*, baffi (for man or animal, = "moustache"); basette *or* fedine (for hair of man's cheek only).
4 *A cat's*, quelli di un gatto. (*Quelli* must be expressed.)
8 *Tossing*, gettando.
9 *Devil take the fowls*, al diavolo le galline.
20 *Stood on guard*, fu messa di guardia *or* fece la guardia.

XLVII

3 *To mistake for*, prendere per *or* confondere con.

5 *At his . . . pace*, con il suo . . . passo.

6 *To push on*, spronare ("to spur": used for a horse and fig. for a person.)

10 *Love of patronage*, desiderio di agire da protettore *or* desiderio di proteggere. (The noun *protezione* cannot be used, as it has a meaning of either receiving or giving patronage.)

11 *Handsome*, bello *or* magnanimo.

12 *Handsome deeds*, buone azioni.

15 *Young man*, giovanotto.

18 *Much*, molto che *or* molte cose che (and Subj.).

19 *Which are said to be worth*, che si dice che valga la pena di. (Impersonal construction in Italian.)

20 *Within easy reach*, facilmente accessibili.

20 *On a bicycle*, in bicicletta.

XLVIII

3 *Intended*, promessa sposa (*wife* understood).

5 *To be at some pains to*, sforzarsi di.

7 *To fling oneself away upon*, sprecarsi con.

8 *Quite*, proprio. (See XXXVI, 7.)

9 *The unexpectedness of the whole affair*, l'intera faccenda era inaspettata.

11 *Would not hear of it*, non voleva sentirne parlare.

13 *Easy to manage*, facile da trattare *or* facile a trattarsi.

13 *I could do nothing with him*, non riuscivo a convincerlo *or* non riuscivo a smuoverlo (coll.) *or* egli era irremovibile.

16 *Would make him more bent on*, lo avrebbe spinto di più a (Past Cond., see Note to II, 11).

16 *To have one's way*, fare di testa sua *or* fare come si vuole.

17 *To please oneself*, agire secondo il suo gusto.

18 *To miss*, non incontrare *or* non vedere (in the sense of "to fail to meet". See XXIX, 8).

26 *As soon as you have learned*, appena avrai appreso. (Future Perfect = "will have learned".)

XLIX

1, 2 *Came down, rose, might.* (Imp.)
2 *Anywhere at all*, dovunque.
3 *To escape*, salvarsi da (in the sense of "to avoid").
4 *To stamp to pieces*, calpestare e ridurre in pezzi.
6 *Would help him*, lo aiutava. (The Italian Imperfect translates the English "would" in the sense of "wanted to", as here, or "used to".)
7 *It was away from him*, ne rimase senza.
8 *In the dawn*, all'alba.
12 *To let the fiddle out of one's hands*, separarsi dal violino.
15 *Before she was done*, prima di darsi per vinta.
20 *To go shopping*, andare a fare la spesa (when buying food. To buy things other than food is *fare le spese*.)

L

3 *Home-made*, fatto in casa.
3 *Tapping one foot*, battendo il tempo con un piede.
5 *At length*, alla fine.
6 *To practise*, esercitarsi in.
6 *Such songs as*, tutti i canti che.
7 *To annoy*, dare fastidio a *or* far arrabbiare. (The Italian *annoiare* means "to bore".)
8 *He would . . . set me*, mi trovava. (Imp. See XLIX, 6.)
11 *To the attic*, in soffitta.
11 *Stealing the cream*, mentre ruba la panna. (The Pres. Part. is translated by *mentre* and the Indicative, as it has here the force of a temporal clause. If, however, a free rendering of the idea is preferred, "like a cat caught stealing the cream" may be translated by the corresponding Italian idiomatic phrase *come uno colto in flagrante*.)

15, 16 *In looking . . . in buying*, guardando . . . comprando. (Italian Gerund with something of the force of the Latin ablative Gerund.)

17 *Herself*, per sè.

19 *So long as*, se *or* purchè (and Subj.).

24 *For him to be out*, a non trovarlo in casa.

LI

14 *I ought . . . to have celebrated*, avrei dovuto celebrare. (See XLV, 21.)

15 *By being*, con l'essere. (Infinitive used as a noun.)

17 *I knew*, che avvertii *or* di cui fui conscio. (See Note to VIII, 14.)

18 *Official*, funzionario. (*Ufficiale* means an officer in the Forces.)

18 *Displeased by*, spiacente per *or* scontento di.

24 *Fleecy white clouds*, nuvolette bianche.

LII

2 *Quite still*, perfettamente fermo.

3 *To set off*, mettersi in cammino.

4 *To ride*, andare *or* venire in bicicletta, a cavallo, etc. In this case, "riding" is *che veniva*. (See XIII, 7.)

8 *Away*, distante *or* a una distanza di.

11 *Stopping*, di essermi fermato (= "having stopped").

11, 12 *In the day-time . . . at night*, di giorno . . . di notte.

15 *Though*, tuttavia *or* però. (At the beginning of the clause.)

22 *Either . . . or*, nè . . . nè (in a negative phrase).

26 *Shut up*, silenzio *or Imperative of* tacere.

26 *What's the use of talking about it?* A che serve parlarne?

LIII

2 *To open upon the street*, dare sulla strada.

8 *Would talk*, eravamo soliti parlare *or* parlavamo. (See
XLIX, 6.)

12 *Sounded to me like the beating of drums*, mi sembrava come
un suono di tamburi.

14 *To spring to one's feet*, balzare in piedi.

17 *To come nearer and nearer*, avvicinarsi sempre di più.

19 *What it meant*, quello che voleva dire *or* ciò che voleva
dire.

LIV

1 *Sitting-room*, sala da soggiorno *or* il soggiorno.

9 *To raise one's hat*, levarsi il cappello a *or* scappellarsi a.

13 *Would be robbed*, sarebbe stato privato. (Past Cond. See
Note to II, 11.)

15, 16 *Could . . . could*, avrebbe potuto.

18 *In the old days*, in passato.

18 *Never . . . any more*, non . . . mai più.

20 *In saying*, nel dire.

22 *To go on business*, andarvi per affari. ("There", understood in English, must be expressed in Italian.)

25 *To prove*, riuscire (in the sense of "to turn out").

27 *Not nearly so easy*, neppure lontanamente così facili.

LV

2 *This greatest of all oceans*, quest'oceano, il più grande di
tutti.

3 *Right*, proprio. (See XXXVI, 7.)

3 *To lie*, giacere (of anything which is still; also of human
beings when they are dead or injured or asleep. See
XXIII, 12.)

13 *On every single,* proprio su ciascuna.
20 *Three times a week,* tre volte alla settimana. (Similar expressions of time are translated by *a* and the definite article: e.g. £30 a month, *trenta sterline al mese;* twice a year, *due volte all'anno.*)
21 *Few and far between,* molto rare.
23 *Something going on,* qualche cosa.
24 *As I get older,* invecchiando *or* con l'andare degli anni *or* col passare degli anni.
28 *At top speed,* in gran fretta.

LVI

4 *Card,* biglietto da visita.
5 *By saying,* col dire.
7 *In his doorway,* sulla porta.
10 *To earn one's bread,* guadagnarsi la vita *or* guadagnarsi da vivere *or* guadagnarsi il pane.
10 *That I did,* dì sì.
12, 13 *I was not, I did so,* non lo ero, lo facevo. (*Lo* is the necessary complement of both verbs.)
14 *He turned upon his heel,* mi voltò le spalle.
17 *That he would have heard,* che egli avesse sentito. ("Would" here is the equivalent of a past tense "had heard", with an idea of probability expressed in Italian by the Subj.)
18 *Was,* è stato. (Perf., like all other Indicative past tenses in this passage.)
25 *They are talked of,* si parla di loro. (Reflexive *si.*)
26 *Given* (= "they are given". See Note to XLV, 17).
27 *To be one,* essere un'attrice *or* essere una di loro. (*Una* by itself is too vague.)
27 *When I grow up,* quando sarò grande.

LVII

4 *To take up one's residence*, prendere alloggio *or* alloggiarsi.

6 *Ever*. (Not to be translated.)

7 *Younger . . . by four or five years*, più giovane di quattro o cinque anni.

9 *To detail at full length*, elencare dettagliatamente *or* elencare nei particolari.

10 *To bring accusations*, fare accuse.

11 *Should* (= "if". Conditional sentence. See Note to XLII, 16).

14 *The letter having miscarried*, mentre la lettera andò perduta *or* essendo andata perduta la lettera.

15 *Lord Byron was known*, si dice che Lord Byron.

16 *Opening lines*, primi versi.

22 *However long*, per quanto lungo.

24 *To learn*, informarsi di *or* sentire. (*Sentire* is used very much in Italian to express the impressions made by a physical sensation like hearing, smelling, feeling: e.g. *sentire un rumore* (see XXIII, 8), *un profumo, un dolore, un sapore*, etc. Figuratively: *sentire gioia, tristezza, interesse*, etc.)

27 *To learn*, apprendere (a piece of news. *Imparare* is to acquire knowledge by study or experience.)

LVIII

2 *Afforded me*, mi dava *or* mi procurava.

7 *To procure sympathy with*, far sì (= così) che altri simpatizzassero con *or* destare in altri simpatia per.

12 *To be at home*, sentirsi a casa sua *or* sentirsi nel proprio elemento.

15 *The spirit moved me*, mi venne in mente di *or* mi sentii trasportato a.

19 *To frighten away one's night's sleep*, tenere uno sveglio per la paura *or* tenere uno sveglio dalla paura.

22 *To leave one's friends behind*, separarsi dai propri amici.
25 *Crossing*, traversata (in the sense of "sea-passage").
26 *Than it really is*, di quanto non sia. (*Non* is pleonastic.)

LIX

1 *To draw to a close*, terminare.
5 *To have some drinks*, bere qualcosa.
5 *To lead the way*, fare strada.
10 *In number*, in tutto.
11 *Presently*, poco dopo.
16 *Peculiar*, strano *or* fuori dell'ordinario. (The Italian *peculiare* means "confined to" or "restricted to".)
17 *Than usual*, del normale.
22 *The chance that*, il caso che (and Imp. Subj.).

LX

1 *A bridal couple*, una coppia di sposini.
4 *Any longer*, più a lungo *or* di più. ("Any" before a comparative is not translated: e.g. any faster, *più rapidamente*.)
5 *To be fond of*, piacere. (See IV, 3.)
7 *If she went to hell*, anche se avesse dovuto andare all'inferno.
12 *Proper*, vero.
16 *Felt*, era. (*Sentire* cannot be used here. See LVII, 24.)
18 *If he went to bed, sleep would go*, se fosse andato a letto, il sonno se ne sarebbe andato via. (Plup. Subj. and P. Cond. as the condition expressed by the if-clause is relating to past time. See Note to XLII, 16.)
19 *To sink deep into it*, per abbandonarvisi completamente *or* per lasciarvisi sommergere.
21 *Seductively*, in modo attraente *or* in modo allettante.
23 *The . . . flaming*, le fiamme *or* il fiammeggiare. (In line 15 "flaming" is *fiammeggiante*, Pres. Part. with the force of an adjective.)

116

LXI

6 *In the doorway*, nel vano della porta.

7 *More than*, più di quanto (and Subj.).

7 *Anything human*, ogni altro essere umano. (*Ogni* is always singular and indeclinable.)

8 *Tied my tongue*, mi fece ammutolire *or* mi rese incapace di parlare.

10 *My*. (Not to be translated.)

13 *To mention*, nominare. (See XLII, 1.)

14 *To grow afraid*, cominciare ad aver paura.

16 *How far is it to . . .?* A che distanza si trova . . .? *or* Quanto dista . . .? *or* Quanto c'è da qui a . . .?

23 *To be out of one's way*, essere fuori strada.

25 *To reach*, arrivare a.

28 *Round*. (Not to be translated.)

30 *What had become of her*, cosa ne era di lei.

30 *On arriving back*, ritornando.

4 *There are hundreds of them!* Ce ne sono delle centinaia! (*Cento* is a hundred; *un centinaio* is approximately a hunddred; *delle centinaia*, feminine plural of *centinaio*. See also II, 7.)

5 *Like that*, così *or* in quel modo.

5 *Not to care*, non importare. (Same construction as *piacere*. See IV, 3.)

7 *To go too far*, passare il limite. *Much too far*, di molto.

8 *Over and over again*, tante volte.

9 *Mumbling as if to himself*, come borbottando fra sè.

12 *No sooner*, appena.

17 *To pass by*, passar via *or* passar oltre.

17 *To take no notice of*, non far caso a *or* non fare attenzione a.

21 *To talk to each other*, parlare l'un l'altro *or* parlare l'uno all'altro.

2 *To enlarge their minds*, arricchire la mente *or* ampliare il proprio orizzonte.

13 *Brilliance*, brio ed efficacia.

13 *Eldest*, il più grande.

17 *To hear somebody going on*, sentire uno che continua a parlare *or* sentire uno continuare a parlare.

20 *It is good*, è bello *or* fa piacere.

25 *So to say*, per così dire.

28 *To pass by*, oltrepassare.

30 *For having made you acquainted with them*, per averteli fatti conoscere (tu) *or* per averglieli fatti conoscere (lei).

LXIV

1 *By*, con *or* per mezzo di.

3 *So far as*, per quanto.

5 *To be of age to look after oneself*, raggiungere un'età in cui si è capaci di fare da sè *or* raggiungere un'età in cui si può provvedere a sè stessi.

5 *As early as may be*, il più presto possibile.

6 *Boarding school*, collegio.

10 *To be dependent on*, dipendere finanziariamente da (in the sense of "being supported by").

14 *At their own option*, a loro scelta. ("It is at their own option", *sta a loro*.)

14 *Whether or no they maintain*, se mantenere . . . o no *or* se mantenere o no . . .

15 *With you*, per voi.

17 *To be rooted*, avere radici.

21 *We are often told*, ci si dice spesso. (See Note to XLV, 17.)

22 *To depend on*, dipendere da (in the sense of "to be contingent on").

23 *What you mean by*, quello che si intende per *or* ciò che si intende per.

25 *At best,* al massimo *or* nel migliore dei casi.
28 *And that, more than anything else, is the . . . ?* e non è quello,
   più di ogni altra cosa, il . . . ?

LXV

1 *The major himself,* il maggiore stesso *or* lo stesso maggiore
  or proprio il maggiore.
1 *To make one's appearance,* comparire.
5 *To see his back,* visto da dietro.
11 *Both . . . and,* sia . . . che *or* tanto . . . che *or* tanto . . .
   quanto.
20 *Having a liking for,* poichè gli piaceva *or* poichè aveva un
   debole per.
20 *Polite life,* la gran vita *or* la vita elegante.
21 *Belonging to it,* che l'accompagnano.
22 *Could she have known,* se avesse saputo.
23 *What kind of people,* che razza di gente *or* che genere di
   persone.
26 *To happen to pass,* passare per caso davanti a *or* capitare
   di passare davanti a. (*Capitare di,* same construction as
   piacere. See IV, 3.)
28 *Whether I liked it or not,* sia che (and Subj.) o no.
36 *Just,* proprio (in the sense of "exactly, precisely").

LXVI

2 *Even though,* anche se.
5 *Conveniences,* comodità.
5 *To be,* come.
8 *To set men to work,* far lavorare gli uomini.
11 *To linger,* sussistere *or* esistere (in the sense of "to con-
   tinue to exist").
12 *About this time,* circa in questo periodo di tempo.
12 *A neighbouring squire,* un signorotto del vicinato.

12 *Referred the following difficulty to Mr. Austen's decision*, sottopose questo problema al Sig. Austen.
14 *Do tell us*, ce lo dica, per favore.
19 *A round oath*, una bella imprecazione *or* una sonora imprecazione.
21 *To pull up*, correggere *or* contradire.
22 *That's neither here nor there*, non è il caso di discutere.
34 *He would rather . . . than*, preferirebbe . . . piuttosto che.
35 *Any*, qualsiasi.

LXVII

1 *Is there another way up?* Si può salire da un'altra parte?
3 *To have thought of that*, pensarci.
7 *That way*, da lì *or* da quella parte.
8 *Here!* Ecco!
9 *Torch*, lampadina.
9 *You'd better*, faresti meglio a.
11 *To think hard*, pensare intensamente *or* pensare profondamente.
12 *To sound*, sembrare.
14 *Her curtains drawn open*, le tende aperte.
17 *To be engaged on*, essere impegnato in *or* essere occupato in.
18 *He neither smoked himself, nor allowed smoking*, nè fumava lui, nè permetteva che si fumasse.
20 *To go out of doors*, uscire all'aperto *or* uscire fuori.
24 *To wait on*, servire.
26 *Joint with vegetables*, carne con verdure *or* carne con contorno.
27 *Left-overs*, avanzi.

LXVIII

1 *It's no use*, è inutile che (and Subj.).
6 *A bit*, neppure un po' *or* nemmeno un po'. (*Neppure or nemmeno* are required as second negative.)

7 *To cry about,* da piangere *or* di cui piangere.
8 *Half laughing,* con un mezzo sorriso.
14 *To cry about it,* piangerne *or* piangere per questo.
18 *Wild,* ansiosa (in the sense of "full of desire").
23 *Misery,* sofferenza. (*Miseria* in Italian means "lack of money".)

LXIX

1 *Made his way down her stairs,* scese le scale della casa di lei.
4 *On the way,* per via.
11 *To slip into his pocket,* mettersela facilmente in tasca.
24 *To run back home,* ritornare di corsa a casa.
27 *To keep,* trattenere.
31 *Just look at it!* Ma guardalo!

LXX

2 *To pack,* mettere.
3 *To set forth,* uscire a *or* andare a.
6 *Glad at,* contenta di.
7 *Gratified by,* lusingate da.
7 *In the mood for,* disposte a.
8 *Impossible, they agreed, to have done better,* erano d'accordo che sarebbe stato impossibile fare meglio.
10 *Not more than twenty minutes' walk,* a non più di venti minuti di strada.
13 *First-rate,* di prima categoria.
15 *Why,* davvero.
17 *I'm going to . . . ,* penso proprio che (and Future).
20 *The children being in bed,* messi a letto i bambini.
21 *Keen appetite,* grand'appetito *or* forte appetito.
25 *On reaching,* arrivata a.
29 *People to have to wait for me,* farmi aspettare dalla gente.
32 *To look up,* alzare gli occhi *or* sollevare lo sguardo.
35 *Looked as though,* sembrava che (and Subj.).

 2 *Downward*, in discesa. ("Upward", *in salita.*)

 4 *To the side*, di fianco.

10 *I say*, ma dico *or* insomma *or* perbacco.

11 *Drawing his hand . . . across*, che si passava la mano . . . su.

13 *At the door*, sulla porta.

13 *A stranger*, una sconosciuta.

14 *I'm sure*, davvero *or* veramente.

17 *You're one*, tu sei uno di loro.

22 *A good fire*, un bel fuoco.

23 *After driving up here*, dopo aver guidato fin quassù.

26 *Goodness knows*, Dio solo sa.

27 *Careless about writing*, pigro nello scrivere.

28 *To be anxious*, stare in pensiero.

30 *Without meaning to be*, senza intenzione di esserlo.

31 *If he turned up*, se si facesse vedere.

31 *Without letting us know*, senza farcelo sapere.

32 *I should expect him to do*, da aspettarsi da lui *or* che io mi aspetterei da lui.

34 *Back*, ancora.

LXXII

 2 *Had been preparing*, si era preparato.

 2 *For so long*, da così tanto tempo.

 3 *It was actually here*, era arrivato veramente.

 8 *To care*, importare di. (See LXII, 5.)

13 *Saying*, che diceva. (See XLIV, 16.)

14 *Thought.* (Imp.)

14 *Out there*, lì dov'era.

17 *Closely written pages*, pagine scritte fitte fitte.

18 *Was*, avvenne *or* era avvenuto.

22 *Just*, soltanto (in the sense of "only").

25 *To spoil the fun*, guastare la festa.

26 *To get worse and worse*, peggiorare sempre di più.

27 *To clear*, rasserenarsi.

27 *For the time being*, per ora.
28 *Without your having to*, senza che voi dobbiate *or* senza che tu debba.

LXXIII

4 *As if*, come per.
5 *Heaven knows*, Dio solo lo sa.
8 *To sink down*, buttarsi *or* lasciarsi andare. (*Sul letto or sulla poltrona or sulla sedia*, etc., must be expressed.)
8 *To bury one's face*, nascondere la faccia.
16 *With neither . . . nor*, senza nè . . . nè.
17 *Self-control*, controllo di sè.
18 *So much as*, neppure.
20, 21 *Back staircase, back door*, scala di servizio, porta di servizio.
21 *To let oneself out*, uscire.
33 *The sooner we are back the better*, più presto torniamo, meglio è.

LXXIV

1 *To turn to stone*, diventare di pietra *or* impietrire.
4 *Writing*, scrittura.
7 *A thick enclosure*, un grosso incartamento.
11 *A queer feeling*, una strana sensazione.
13 *So did I*, io feci lo stesso.
14 *The latch of the door give*, la maniglia della porta girare.
18 *Opposed to*, contrari a.
22 *To be fortunate in*, essere fortunato di.
24 *The same as those*, gli stessi che.
25 *To lay stress on*, dare rilievo a *or* mettere in evidenza.
27 *By*, da parte di.

3 *Streets baked in an arid glare of sunlight,* strade infuocate dall'arida, accecante luce del sole.

4 *To powder,* impolverare.

7 *To point out,* far notare.

9 *To happen to pass in or out of,* per caso entrare o uscire da.

10 *When he chose,* quando voleva.

11 *It was not until . . . that,* soltanto quando . . .

14 *There . . . lay,* su questo . . . si basava.

17 *To lay bare one's plans to,* mettere a nudo i suoi piani davanti a.

21 *Less,* di più. (The exact opposite word in Italian!)

24 *At a fair speed,* a buona velocità.

25 *Came off and rolled away on its own account,* uscì fuori e rotolò per conto suo.

26 *To fall over sideways,* rovesciarsi da un lato.

27 *In a straight line,* in linea retta.

28 *In bringing it to a stop,* a farla fermare.

29 *Had narrowly missed a man,* per poco non aveva colpito.

30 *To congratulate on,* congratularsi per.

32 *To see,* assicurarsi.

33 *To fasten securely,* fissare fermamente.

6 *Her guess,* l'indovinare.

10 *A kind of,* una specie di.

15 *To cause someone much thought,* dare a uno molto da pensare.

19 *Unnoticed,* senza essere notati.

20 *Played a part,* entravano *or* erano comprese.

21 *To manage,* mandare ad effetto *or* riuscire in.

22 *Any of them,* qualsiasi di questi piani. (*Piani* expressed.)

27 *There are no quiet corners left,* non ci sono (*or* siano) rimasti degli angoli tranquilli.
28 *There is always an alternative route to be found,* si può sempre trovare un'altra strada.
29 *It does take a little longer,* ci si mette un po' di più *or* ci vuole un po' di più. ("To take" applied to time is *metterci* inflected, or *ci vuole*, third person sg. and pl.)
33 *The picturesqueness,* le qualità pittoresche.

LXXVII

2 *To taste nothing but,* non mangiare altro che *or* mangiare soltanto.
3 *Draught,* sorso (of any liquid).
4 *By the roadside,* lungo la strada.
8 *More alone than,* più solo di come non (and Subj.).
9 *Tired with,* stanco per.
18 *To make someone worse,* far peggiorare qualcuno.
21 *At the bottom,* ai piedi (of a hill or a mountain).
22 *To beg of,* chiedere l'elemosina a.
23 *Took any notice of him,* lo notarono *or* si accorsero di lui.
26 *Laden with,* carichi di.
30 *I am afraid,* purtroppo *or* disgraziatamente.

LXXVIII

1 *To get on well with,* andare d'accordo con *or* intendersela con.
8 *Anything of the sort,* niente di simile.
12 *To be lonely and homesick,* sentirsi soli e pieni di nostalgia.
15 *Being friendly in its fashion,* il suo modo di mostrarsi amico.
21 *To come up,* crescere.

LXXIX

2 *Appointment*, appuntamento (in the sense of "meeting").

3 *Silk factory*, setificio.

5 *To look*, apparire *or* sembrare.

7 *At the counter*, allo sportello.

10, 15 *Looking*, ed appariva. (Make it into a coordinate clause.)

15 *Miserable*, triste *or* avvilita *or* abbattuta.

18 *Waited for*, aspettò che (and Subj.).

28 *He ought to know*, dovrebbe saperlo.

30 *To regret it*, pentirsene.

LXXX

2 *On an errand*, a fare una commissione.

3 *About . . . distant*, a una distanza di circa . . .

3 *By the road*, andando per strada. (The other appearances of "by" in line 4 may be translated by *per*.)

5 *The evenings closed in early*, si faceva scuro presto *or* le serate si erano accorciate.

5 *Were thick and misty*, c'era molta nebbia *or* c'era nebbia fitta.

7 *Bed-ridden*, allettato *or* costretto a letto.

8 *Had done*, feci. (P.Def.)

9 *Earlier by an hour*, un'ora più presto.

10 *I took the decision . . . into my own hands*, decisi da me.

13 *It looked dark and gloomy enough*, il tempo era proprio scuro e tetro.

18 *Exactly similar*, perfettamente uguali.

22 *She had only left herself twenty minutes or so*, le erano rimasti soltanto circa venti minuti di tempo.

26 *Out of action*, fuori uso.